A Cockney Rosebud

*A bittersweet journey
in the midst of the life and community
of an East End of London family
(circa 1920 – 1960)*

JOSIE BRUCE

Copyright © 2024 Josie Bruce
All rights reserved.

No part of this book may be reproduced, or stored in a retrieval system, or transmitted in any form or by any means, electronic, mechanical, photocopying, recording, or otherwise, without express written permission of the publisher.

Based on True Life Events

1

The distinctive cry of a newborn brought not only new life to Gold Street, Stepney, East London on the 16th of May, 1920, but also the hope that the horrors and deprivation of a world war would continue to fade. A post-World-War-I baby, conceived when her father was released from the Royal Navy into Civvy Street, she enchanted and sparkled the pallor of her surroundings with mesmeric wisps of blond hair and piercing azure eyes that reflected the heavens above, as if heralding a bright new world. Her limbs were milky white and surprisingly long, with fingers that reached out and played in the air. Her parents named her Rosie.

A COCKNEY ROSEBUD

The procreative instinct was immense at war's end. The war had claimed the lives of 888,246 British men and boys with 1,663,435 wounded, and it was impossible to walk the streets of London without meeting men with only one arm or leg, disfigured, blind or with only one eye—and they were the demobbed souls who were able to step out from their living quarters. The aftermath of such a bloody, hand-to-hand combat war had decimated the close-knit docklands community into which Rosie was now born. Parents had lost sons, wives had lost husbands, and families grieved for uncles, nephews, and cousins. An inestimable loss of breadwinners. A close neighbour that Rosie would soon know lost five sons. Women did not go to work; they raised the children and kept the house—it was the men who brought home the money. For those returning home, already weighted with trauma and dreadful memories, the docks had almost closed down and prospects for the injured and disabled were dire. How would this treasured 'rosebud' thrive and bloom? High rents—through private landlords— subletting and overcrowding, living in cramped, often unsanitary conditions with just a shared outdoor toilet, and poor diet, ensured poor health and diminished prospects throughout the community.

It was 1920, less than two years after World War I had ended, but with the joyous return of the surviving men and the subsequent rise in the birth rate, an extravaganza of creativity and potential greatness would be underpinned, as existence transformed into living once again. Legendary actors Yul Brynner, Montgomery Clift, Walter Mattau, Mickey Rooney and Shelley Winters were born that year, together with author P. D. James, musician Ravi Shankar and the singer Peggy Lee. In London, *The Planets* by Gustav Holst premiered; Joan of Arc was canonised as a saint, whilst in sharp contrast, the USA enacted the 'Prohibition of Alcohol.' For Gold Street, Stepney, and the docklands community, survival was still all consuming.

2

Rosie's father, Edmund James, was born in 1889 in Stratford, London. He was the eldest of six children, three boys and three girls. However, one brother, Henry, died aged only two from whooping cough in 1892. Edmund worked as a barman but went to sea at sixteen, joining The Royal Navy as a stoker but progressing to chief petty officer by the time of his release. Life and work in the Navy brought out the best in him—he was not afraid of work but suffered from a bad chest, and the sea air was therapeutic. Later, life in Civvy Street would not be as rewarding. He was of medium build (Navy records show him as 5'6" tall), stocky, fair-haired, with a fresh complexion, and he had a sailor's twinkle in his blue eyes. He signed up in November 1905 but would stay on for fourteen years, working on minesweepers during World War I.

Edmund had a talent. Spending so much time away from home and onboard ship, he amused himself by learning magician secrets. He amassed a big trunk of props and could do some marvellous tricks. Children loved it. A walking stick that turned into a flag, card tricks, coloured handkerchiefs that he could screw up slowly in his hands and then open his palms, which would be empty, a ball that could float between his outstretched hands, and another ball that he could make disappear. He perfected the tricks and, with a poker face, he would extract their pennies from them. He didn't give them back.

Edmund married in 1912 aged twenty-three. The wedding was a grand affair at St. Dunstan's Church in Stepney High Street, which was known as the 'Church of the High Seas' and had strong connections to everything seafaring. Fishing nets would bedeck the church at Harvest Festival. Above the main entrance door, there was a symbolic carving of a ship. Printed documents from the church records, covering many centuries, show the red ensign flag of British passenger and merchant ships adorning the top of the church tower with pride.

Although it would sustain bomb damage during World War II [1939-1945], a church had already existed on the site before the 10th century. After a devastating fire had destroyed large parts of the church in 1901, it underwent extensive repairs with restorations funded by a public appeal. For a poor parish to collect enough money testifies to the importance of the church to the locality, to the seamen, and their families. Centuries of burials in the huge graveyard serve to remind of disasters, such as plague, in addition to natural deaths. However, after burials ceased in 1854, a programme of gravestone clearance was undertaken and, in 1886, the graveyard was reopened as a public garden and a more fitting backdrop to wedding ceremonies that honoured the living. Rosie's maternal grandparents, Robert and Sarah, were among the first to enjoy their wedding celebrations in the new gardens with their marriage taking place at St. Dunstan's in April 1886.

The *wedding banns*—an obligatory proclamation of the intended marriage recorded and confirmed by the church—list Edmund's address as Wellesley Street, just a hop away from his future bride, Lily Eleanor, who lived in lodgings in Cordelia Square with her parents and her sister. The marriage certificate gave his occupation as 'on the High Seas'. As Rosie grew into an inquisitive little girl, finding the certificate in a kitchen drawer amongst insurance policies and the like, those four words would evoke striking images of a billowing flotilla, high on the waves, with her father, in full dress uniform, on the deck repelling pirates and 'ne'er do wells.' Age and maturity would render these images less dramatic and closer to reality of a life 'on the High Seas' with a copious amount of scrubbing the deck and the trademark bell bottoms soaking up the grubby water. Edmund wore his uniform 'whites' at the wedding, and a big gun carriage was pulled along with an indulgent degree of pomp. A cherished photo of the occasion was on permanent display on the mantelpiece in Gold Street. His future wife, and Rosie's mother, Lily Eleanor's occupation was given as an 'ERS Tape Gummer', which to the mind of a child, did not sound at all exciting!

Rosie would never know how they met, but a sailor on leave, in uniform and with a twinkle in his eye, would be known to every unwed girl in the surrounding streets, like a colony of ants stalking a discarded potato crisp. Lily Eleanor was not a beauty. She was of medium height and build, had dark hair that she wore in a bun and dark, serious eyes. She had little tolerance of frivolities. She was, however, a confident young woman with good manners, poise, and a neat appearance. Two years after their wedding, in 1914, their first daughter, named Lily (Blanche) after her mother, was born. Lily Blanche took after her mother with dark hair and dark eyes but had the misfortune to inherit a weak heart gene from her father's family, which would manifest itself in later years.

With her husband away at sea, Lily Eleanor had to step up at quite a young age to run the house and bring up a baby. Daughter Lily Blanche spent a lot of time within the close family unit of her paternal grandmother, Elizabeth Emily. She quickly became a favourite. She would entertain her Aunt Roseada (who was frail from illness) and later run small errands for her granny. Lily Eleanor did not visit Elizabeth Emily unless invited. Lily Eleanor's immediate family was not close knit. She was born in January 1888 and was closely followed by a brother, who sadly died aged only four years. Child deaths were common in those days, particularly from childhood diseases such as measles. She had a much younger sister by fifteen years, Elizabeth Florence (Bessie). By coincidence, one of Edmund's sisters was also named Elizabeth Florence. Florence was a popular name in this era due to the work of Florence Nightingale, who in those days was regarded as a 'medical angel'.

The family struggled to make ends meet and moved lodgings frequently. Lily Eleanor was relieved on her marriage to be able to put down roots and utilise the skills she had learned from her family's difficult financial times and manage her own economy. And she had a husband in full-time work. Prospects would improve for her parents during World War I when they became licensees of a pub and began to thrive, fitting into that world like the final pieces of a jigsaw. The constant upheaval of moving, finding work, interrupted schooling and lack of funds might have contributed to a dysfunctional family unit. Lily Eleanor's parents were unable to express love, support, and belonging to their daughter, and this resulted in Lily Eleanor understanding this as normal behaviour which she passed down to the next generation. She didn't know how to form a relationship with her mother-in-law and avoided potential (mutual) discomfort by deciding that Elizabeth Emily did not warm to her. After all, if her own mother didn't enjoy her company, why would her mother-in-law?

3

Edmund's immediate family, who were close neighbours in Gold Street, were talented and creative. His mother, Elizabeth Emily, was the matriarch. Born in Poplar in 1868, she worked as a domestic servant for a family in West Ham from the age of fourteen. She married William, seven years older, in 1888. William did physically demanding jobs and he died soon after Rosie was born. Short but wiry, with dark hair in a neat bun and a healthy complexion, Elizabeth Emily was practical and forthright. She knitted profusely. She was a natural cook and honed her talents to progress from a domestic to chef at a prestigious gentlemen's club in central London.

Edmund's three sisters, all younger than him, lived with his mother. Elsie Martha was born in 1897. She got engaged but lost her fiancé in World War I and never married. She was a self-taught Gold Embroidress and embroidered the epaulettes of uniforms by hand, working from home. The pride she took in her work was evidenced by the jacket framework, proudly displayed in her room, and covered in soft white leather, which she would caress and smooth as she positioned each uniform jacket. She was also an accomplished musician and music teacher. She played and taught piano, having qualified as a piano teacher, with her certificates prominently displayed on the wall. Absorbed in her embroidery, her mellow singing tone would infuse the air, and the uniform jacket, as if the moisture of her gentle breathing imparted her unrequited love into the fabric.

Elizabeth Florence (Lizzie) was born in 1893, married in 1918 and lived upstairs in their mother's house. She had a son, Norman, born only three months earlier than Rosie, who would also develop musical talents. By the age of eighteen, he would form his own dance band and perform locally in social clubs, parties and at weddings.

Edmund's third sister, Roseada, was born in 1900 and had a sad life dogged by a serious heart condition. She spent her days resting on a chaise longue but was able to absorb the company, bustle, and love of her family around her. Her life would be cut short at the age of twenty-nine before she had the opportunity to blossom.

4

With her husband at sea from their marriage in 1912 to 1919 (when Edmund was demobbed from the Navy) and Lily Blanche safely with her granny, Lily Eleanor led an almost independent life, but not for her own enjoyment or permissiveness. The routine estrangement from her husband did not fulfil any desire for closeness and companionship, although her upbringing had likely extinguished any spark of real emotional attachment to another human being. Marriage and children were a natural progression, but love and emotion for Lily Eleanor were not. Both tacit and overt expressions of emotion (if they had ever been in her psyche) had been slowly and deliberately stripped away, like a dedicated whittler shaping a realistic human form on the outside but without anything of emotional value within. In contrast, she had a strong sense of duty and community and was canny with money. Unlike many of her neighbours, she received a regular Navy wage—whether her husband was at home or at sea—so she rarely experienced the trauma of not being able to pay her way. She was obsessed with insurance policies—fearing the unknown and unexpected—and the insurance man visited every week, stamping multiple policy books as the pennies were counted. Rents were high and employment could not be guaranteed once Edmund was demobbed. The big old terraced Victorian house they rented in Gold Street cost a guinea a week. Nearly everyone sublet a room or two to make ends meet. There was always an old lady or elderly couple living in a back room at the top of the house, without a blood connection to the householder. Lily Eleanor had a Mr. and Mrs. Lefly lodging with her. Women outlived the men, leaving them old, isolated and often without adequate funds. The householder would look out for the old lady, take in a meal occasionally, and run errands. It was part of community life.

These old houses were big but only functional if one family occupied it. They had one outdoor toilet, at the end of the backyard, an outdoor washhouse for laundry, and running water only in the downstairs kitchen. Anyone renting upstairs rooms had to get fresh water from a stand-by tap in the backyard, use chamber pots in their room at night—and empty them with a trek to the outdoor toilet— use the washhouse for their laundry, and cook on a gas cooker located on the landing outside of their room. The siting of the gas cooker on a landing was routine in those days and preferable to being inside the cramped rented rooms. They would also have to get coal for their fire. All rooms had a fireplace. The fire would be the only means of heating large amounts of water to wash and clean and would be needed even in the warmer months. Their living, sleeping and eating arrangements were confined to one room, the size of which related to what you could afford. The elderly ladies, without family and with little money, had to endure abject loneliness together with worsening health.

Lily Eleanor's house in Gold Street was typical. The houses were terraced on both sides of the street. An entrance door off the pavement, without a front garden or path, opened into a long, tiled hall. The step up to the front door was an overt measure of cleanliness and respectability to the community, and it was scrubbed clean daily and treated with 'Cardinal' red polish, buffing it to a deep red shine. This was a time-consuming task that would become Rosie's daily chore, along with polishing the brass door knocker. There was a big front parlour with a huge window, but the parlour was sacrosanct and only used for special occasions. It had what were called 'Store Curtains', billowing highly patterned nets that met in the middle and heavy velvet curtains to the sides. There was a fireplace in the parlour in which a fire never sat. It was a focal point with a substantial horse and carriage ornament on the mantelpiece, a wedding present to Lily Eleanor and Edmund. In the hearth was a wide fan of coloured paper and, to complete the opulent effect, a big brass fender with brass fire irons—all polished regularly and innocently providing a shrine to their marriage. The furniture was very low to the ground: a leather settee, two chairs (but no table), and a glass display cabinet. With Edmund in the Navy, the glass cabinet displayed some lovely pieces from around the world, and in their bedroom, Lily Eleanor had a big glass 'fountain' ornament from Venice. The parlour housed an upright piano, adorned with candlesticks, and on top, a goldfish in a bowl. Everyone had a goldfish as the 'Rag and Bone man'(someone who touted for old clothes and furniture touring the streets with a horse and cart) always handed a goldfish in a plastic bag filled with water to the clamouring children, if the adults gave him anything. The poor goldfish in Rosie's house would jump out of the bowl but be put back to continue swimming, aimless and alone, its attempts at escape, or more likely suicide, thwarted each time. The front parlour was on the right and the staircase on the left. Under the staircase was a huge cellar and the coal was kept there. Lily Eleanor would buy a ton of coal and, when the coalmen arrived, she would stand to attention and count the bags going in. It was too easy for a bag to 'go missing'.

The room next to the parlour was Edmund and Lily Eleanor's bedroom. Further along the hall corridor was a door that led outside to the backyard and a final door led into the kitchen. This was the hub of the house. A big wooden table (which was regularly scrubbed) and chairs dominated the kitchen near the huge fireplace, in which a fire was always lit. It was needed for warmth, heating of water, and for Lily Eleanor to cook. She had a black iron gas cooker—an oven with gas rings above—but only used it for food storage. She was brought up cooking over an open fire so why change? Progress and change were anathema to Lily Eleanor. The fireplace housed two huge cooking pots and a large kettle, always in use. The kitchen was where everyone washed. As young children, the adults would still be around but, as soon as puberty was reached, the kitchen door was shut for privacy. Once a week, the tin bath would be brought in from the backyard and the younger children would have a bath with water heated on the fire. Liquid soap did not exist and they used Lifebuoy soap for personal hygiene, including hair, and Sunlight soap and soda for washing clothes. No bleach, but there was lye (caustic soda) for deep cleansing. All the strong cotton fabrics of the day boiled up well. The small pieces left from the bars of soap would be boiled to make a new bar to eke out every bit. Cleanliness was very important to Lily Eleanor, and daily washing, followed by clean clothes, was akin to a ritual.

The washhouse was a vital annex. It was in the backyard, which was quite spacious. Her mother-in-law, just a few doors down, grew some lovely flowers in her backyard, including lilies, which were Lily Eleanor's favourite flower. Lily Eleanor grew some tulips one time, but this was a frivolity that did not sit well with more important duties. The washhouse had a coal-fired copper boiler that had to be lit. It was huge with a big metal lid. There was a metal rubbing board, upgraded at some point from wood, and a large wooden mangle. Everything was starched. All the clothes were made of cotton, nothing synthetic. Lily Eleanor was always washing, even by candlelight, and in winter, the washhouse doubled as a drying room.

Beyond the washhouse, at the bottom of the yard and devoid of lighting, was the wooden hut housing the high metal cistern toilet with a wooden seat and a long chain pull. The walls of the washhouse and toilet were whitewashed to help lighten the rooms, but you had to use candles when it was dark.

In the main house, there was gas lighting by lamps on the walls and no one routinely looked at the ceilings, until electric lighting came to the whole of Gold Street around 1930. As the evening drew in, Lily Eleanor was persuaded to switch on the new light in the kitchen. She was terrified. She did not understand what this 'electricity' thing was. Where did it come from, and where did it go? Was it dangerous? Would the house blow up or catch fire? Her fear was genuine, but they had to have light. She stared at the round protuberance on the wall, identified the switch, wiped her hands several times on her apron and, with a strong intake of breath, she closed her eyes and flicked the switch downwards. The instant arc of light, like the sun bursting through a grey cloud, drew their eyes upwards towards the new light hanging from the ceiling and Lily Eleanor gasped in horror as the ceiling was illuminated. As a fiercely houseproud East Ender, seeing a grimy ceiling went to her core. This new-fangled electricity also stunned the spiders, numbed for a few seconds as the light showcased their dangling cobwebs before they scurried off, their previous freedom irrevocably damaged. Lily Eleanor was so upset, the white-wash came out that same evening.

Back in the house, some upstairs rooms were always sublet. At the top of the staircase, on the left, was a small room where, as their family grew, three young children would sleep. Up three more steps and there was a big front room, a smaller room to the back, and a gas cooker on the landing. The front room was sublet regularly, whilst an elderly couple (the Lefly's) lived in the back room for many years. After her husband died, the old lady remained alone until her own death.

5

Such beautiful autumnal colours abounded. The streets of Stepney may have lacked hibernating plant life and birdsong, but the common ground, parks and gardens never failed to delight. The bare branches of the red dogwood, leaves discarded as the new sap prepared to flow, magnificent in their defiance of approaching winter, displayed blood red veins of health and vitality and cocked a snoot at the wind and weather. The yellow forsythia gave an inkling of spring, like a swathe of daffodil petals catching the sunlight. Old wood fell, to be swallowed in time by the damp earth and fallen leaves or collected for firewood by excited children who ran wild and free, inspired by the freedom that only nature can give. Leaves turned brown, copper, and gold, but which fell first? Walk between the trees or on the well-trodden open lands and waterlogged earth squelched underfoot, eerily a second or two behind the action of the boot, and did you hear the low moan at each upward step. Nature is alive, but the wonder is lost on Lily Eleanor. Practical and devoid of emotion, autumn meant warmer clothes and increased laundry. It is November 1921: Rosie is eighteen months old and thriving. Not yet exposed to the wider community, her days are spent in the warm kitchen, watching her mother bustle with everyday chores, outings in the pram for daily supplies—the pram base doubling as a shopping basket—and naps in the bed that she shared with her sister at night. Daily shopping was a must: without fridges, it was impossible to keep meat and dairy products for very long, but there was a meat safe in the backyard, which meant that the most perishable items could be kept at least overnight. Her sister, aged seven, was at school during the day and was welcomed into Granny's on her return, making a close bond difficult to establish between her and Rosie. Her mother was protective of her baby girl, but that was evidenced in warm clothes, good food, and a safe environment. Nourishment of Rosie's soul was lacking: no bedtime stories, no cradle rocking and lullabies and, crucially, rare expressions of love and cuddles. She hardly knew her father. When Edmund finally returned from sea in 1919, the bloom of his reintegration into traditional married life faded too quickly, like the shine on the revered hearth in their parlour: to ensure depth of lustre, it took commitment. But neither was able to compromise. The physical distance between them was turning, albeit slowly, into an emotional chasm. They had dreams of moving to Clacton-on-Sea in Essex when the children were older, and opening an off-licence (liquor store) to sell beer and other alcoholic drinks. Edmund's chest would be eased with beneficial sea air. A second World War would ensure that this would not be fulfilled.

They had been married for nine years, with Edmund at sea for the first seven, and Lily Eleanor was no longer the young woman he had courted and married. By necessity, she had grown in confidence and independence. And, in their limited days and weeks together over the years, he may have realised that his wife was emotionally impaired and unable to pine for his return. Lily Eleanor had coped with loneliness since she was a young child: she ached for praise from her mother but endured criticism, and her father did not intervene. In time, she believed that she was not worthy of being loved and created a persona of ability and confidence, with which she faced the adult world. The whittler(s) had done a grand job and Lily Eleanor would never know true joy and happiness. Her emotional inadequacy had developed from a peccadillo to a tragic flaw.

6

When Edmund was demobbed from the Navy, he secured work in Civvy Street at a time of massive unemployment, jumping at the chance to join his in-laws, Sarah and Robert, at the pub that they ran successfully, The British Queen in Shoreditch. Lily Eleanor's sister, Bessie, worked behind the bar and Bessie's best friend, Eva, was employed as a cleaner. The pub, however, was three miles from Gold Street and his wife. Edmund started as a licensed victuallers' assistant, but due to his previous bar experience, he was soon promoted to manager, which meant long hours and responsibility. Ergo, as the distance was too far to walk home on foot, he often stayed overnight after a long shift. He had a whole day off each Thursday, which he spent with his family in

Gold Street. For Lily Eleanor, this was little change from when he was at sea and, for the children, their father was a welcome visitor who did magic tricks and made them laugh. Edmund coped with the arrangements rather too well: he felt appreciated at the pub and soon developed strong relationships with his in-laws and the cleaner, Eva.

Eva was a timid, subservient woman. Both she and Bessie were regular church-goers, and Eva gave a Sunday School class for the young children. Her family life was challenging: living in a cramped tenement in Shoreditch, one of 13 siblings with no father, a bed-ridden mother, and a brother in a mental health institution who she would visit once a month. Money was very tight. Eva stirred feelings in Edmund that his wife could not, in fact, the two women were opposites. In the pub, he was the 'top man' respected for his position and liked by the customers. His cheeky banter with Eva was mutually admired and, in his heart, he was strutting like a peacock, displaying his masculine colours. Eva was initially innocently coy, and, unlike a peahen, did not have to warn off any rivals. Bessie, his wife's sister, did not seem perplexed: she had rarely seen her sister since Lily Eleanor's marriage to Edmund, and they had never been close. Edmund dampened his ardour when his in-laws (and employers) were present: they did not exude warmth, but did respect the sacred vows of marriage.

Edmund found the double life easy to manage. When performing his magic tricks, he used distraction and deceit to enthral his audiences, so keeping up appearances at home did not challenge him and he found his dalliance with dishonour rather thrilling.

Once again, the distinctive cry of a newborn was heard on Gold Street as Lily Eleanor gave birth to a blonde-haired boy, rather small in build, but a perfect ray of sunshine bringing light to the dark November days of 1921. This birth completed Lily Eleanor and Edmund's family, and new baby boy Edmund Robert (Ted) joined his two sisters, Lily Blanche (aged seven) and Rosie (aged eighteen months). The birth brought joy to the extended families and especially to Granny Elizabeth Emily, whose husband had died, aged only fifty-nine years, a few months earlier: Rosie and Ted would never know their paternal grandfather.

7

Passers-by smiled at the pretty three-year-old skipping along the road, hand clasped tightly in her big sister's hand, blond curls peeking out randomly from her bonnet with a white starched apron securely tied around the waist of her functional dress and a large bib around her neck. This was Rosie's first day at the Baker Street School, following in the footsteps of her mother who attended aged three in 1891.

The school had opened in 1876 but sadly was to close in 1927.

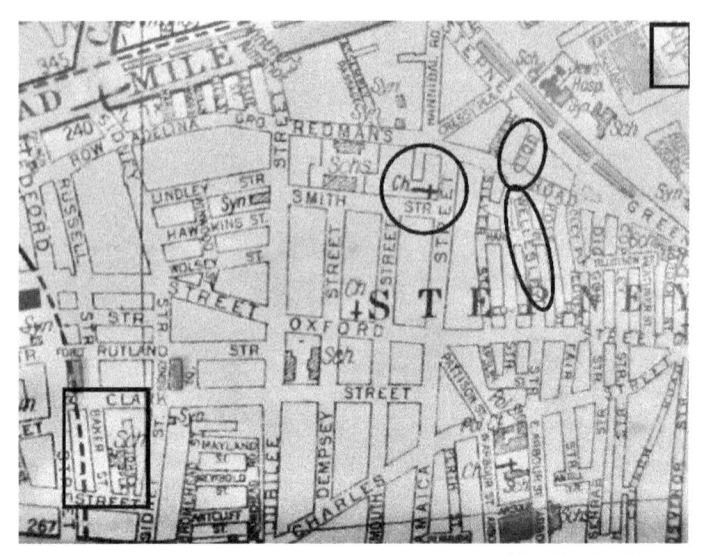

Image by courtesy of www.jewisheastend.com / Philip Walker

Rosie's early world, with its axis in Gold Street, was compact but never confined; out of Gold Street into Jamaica Street, right turn into Clark Street and then a left turn into Baker Street. Everyone she met smiled and said "Hello." In preparation for school, she was measured for sturdy black leather boots—in those days, everyone wore boots. Called 'Russian Boots', they were laced up to the knees and secured with buttons. White cotton socks were worn inside in summer and black socks in winter. Rosie was so proud of her dinky version and felt so grown up. With each skip, she would glance down and giggle at her bouncing feet. In time, she would learn how to do the buttons herself and, in later years, she would go into Granny Elizabeth Emily's house and do Granny's boots up with a button hook as Granny's fingers stiffened with age.

Baker Street School could be likened to a modern-day nursery school. Rosie loved it. Each child had a little desk and chair, a slate board, and a piece of chalk. She took 'tuppence' (two old pennies) a day, which was the fee paid to the school, and included a drink of milk. The children had their little boards, and coloured chalk, and drew, with the helpers' encouragement, as they chattered and laughed. Then, in the afternoon, the desks were turned over and hammocks hung across the legs for the youngsters to have a sleep in. The school did not provide food, and Rosie took bread and jam, or bread and dripping, for her meal. The children were looked after. They had visits from the 'Nit Nurse' to check their hair and were given a daily spoonful of cod liver oil, a prime source of vitamin A. In the 1920s, the idea that vitamin A could strengthen the immune system and help fight infections was developing. Vitamin A supplements became an important public health intervention to reduce mortality among children from infections such as measles. Rosie had no idea that she was part of an important medical initiative as she squeezed her nostrils tight and swallowed the 'goo'.

Life at home was steady and routine. Lily Blanche, now nine years old, had been diagnosed with the hereditary heart weakness from her father's side and was treated with care. She was excused from physical exercise at school. Instead, she spent happy hours in Granny's house, helping with small errands, watching her aunt sew, and listening to the children who came in for piano lessons. Lily Blanche was not musical and had little interest in learning the piano herself. Back at home, Lily Eleanor busied herself with the laundry (in and out of the washhouse and backyard) and preparing the evening meal whilst Rosie and Ted played on the floor in the warm kitchen. Lacking conversation and engagement, Rosie was prone to daydreaming and, if Ted was napping or engrossed in something, she would sit cross-legged by the fire and listen to the trill of the gently boiling kettle whilst immersing her senses in the dancing flames, tilting her head as the flames licked around the fire bricks and disappeared into the abyss of the chimney, her increasingly rosy cheeks glistening against the backdrop of her blond curls.

In those early childhood years, Rosie was clothed, well fed, warm, and safe. Love was expressed by her father (on Thursdays) and her granny Elizabeth Emily and aunts. She did not understand that open expressions of love were absent from her mother—she did not miss what she had never had.

The three children slept in the small room upstairs, with Ted in a big brass cot and the two girls in a bed together. In later years, Ted would be given the room and the bed to himself and Rosie would understand that boys were treated differently. Lily Eleanor would buy a 'put-you-up' bed for the front parlour for Rosie and her sister, whilst (paying) strangers enjoyed the better rooms in the house.

Thursday was their family day; the day their father came. Rosie saw so little of her father in her formative years that she believed he was still in the Navy. Her mother didn't dispel this belief and Rosie was ecstatic when he came home the night before and stayed a whole day. He would scoop both Rosie and Ted up and dance a sailor's jig around the kitchen before sitting in a chair by the fire where the siblings would scramble to get on his lap, simultaneously scared and excited as he tickled them and pretended to be a monster who just might gobble them up. Their laughter would echo from the high ceilings, creating a memory that Rosie could recall at will.

She wished for the day to last and last.

Edmund loved to cook. He had learned to cook while he was in the Navy, which meant that everything he cooked was on a large scale. He made lovely rich soups (pea soup being a family favourite) and stews in the big pots over the fire, summer, and winter. Rosie's mouth would drool when he made his gorgeous steak and kidney pudding with a gleaming white cloth covering the top to perfect the pudding crust. As they ladled their suppers from the pots, Lily Eleanor would say to Rosie, "Take that bowl upstairs" (to the old lady) or "Take that next door." There was always enough and a willingness to share. Edmund also loved to cook eels which no one else in the family would touch but had to endure the preparation and smell. Eels were bought live. Rosie would spend 'eel' days pinching her nose shut and breathing through her mouth. Warm, fed, happy, and feeling like a family—if only for one day a week—the children would chatter away and urge Edmund to do magic tricks, which even their mother enjoyed. The conversations (in front of the children) were light and trivial: the weather, the food prices, aches and pains. Rosie would never learn about her ancestors or her roots or witness true warmth between her parents.

On Thursday evenings, Lily Eleanor and Edmund played cards at a local community hall. They belonged to a Whist Drive Club and often came home with prizes. Lily Eleanor and Edmund were good card players, and perhaps Edmund's 'magician's' face helped! On their return, the children would still be up and Lily Blanche would be back from Granny's. The siblings would then sit on the floor between their parents and talk nineteen-to-the-dozen whilst toasting muffins over the fire on the long toasting fork. They would lick their lips, anticipating the melted butter that would crown the tops. It was indeed a very special day. But if a passer-by had tarried at their downstairs window, they might have caught the sigh of relief as Lily Eleanor extinguished the lights, drew the heavy curtains to signal the close of the day and fell asleep, safe in the knowledge that the next day (with Edmund back at the pub) her independence would be restored.

8

The rainbow arched proudly in the sky, showcasing the brilliant beams of sunlight that danced on the coin in the hand of a small child skipping towards the rainbow and the sweet shop.

Rosie's childhood had defined seasons: she could expect winter (December to March) to be dark, cold, and frosty with snow at Christmas time and perhaps beyond, the crisp white flakes soiling as they touched the coal dust, which was always present on the streets. March would conclude the thaw and commence the house-proud East Enders' nightmare of slush. The children loved to shuffle, splash, and kick about in it. Slush had a consistency of lumpy, icy mashed potato and, when carried into the house under the sturdy boots of the time, left dirty swirling puddles. Of course, children also fell over in the slush, often quite happily.

Spring heralded warmth and new life. Buds on trees, lilies and tulips effortlessly pushing their blades through warming ground and, in the common areas and parks, blades of grass shooting up in abandonment. Summer brought blue skies and sunshine, locals strolling through the streets in lighter cotton clothes, and greeting everyone with a cheerful smile and an "Hello."

The school holidays enabled games of great imagination on the *Mile End Waste*. Discarded prams—no longer safe for infants— made great ships for pirate games, with fallen tree wood as swords, and wooden crates could be turned into homes to play 'mothers and fathers' with large pieces of rag impersonating rather swish curtains, and a blanket for a baby doll. Boys would box barefoot and encouraged by their pals. 'The Waste', as it was colloquially known, was a favourite haunt for children, being not only a huge piece of open common ground where they could run, play and breathe—free from the confines of their cramped homes—but a place of nature, awe, and learning.

Long before Rosie's birth, Mile End Green had been the largest of several commons in the Manor of Stepney and was crossed by what later became, and still is, a major transport link, the *Mile End Road*. During the eighteenth century, the road was busy with merchants and industry, including a brewery and distillery, but as the merchants moved away, the remaining community—which was poor and predominantly Jewish—swelled, and 'The Waste' became a hub for religious and political meetings, continuing into the nineteenth and early twentieth centuries.

The 'Band of Hope' was notable and, when meeting in the churches, they included Christian teachings. It was a temperance movement founded in Leeds in 1874. Its mission was to enable daily life without the crutch of alcohol, a challenging mission as this had been the norm for centuries. Its main objective was to teach children the importance and principles of sobriety and teetotalism. In Queen Victoria's Jubilee year (1897), the estimated membership was 3,238,323 and growing. Members signed the 'pledge' of the Band of Hope: *'I, the undersigned, do agree that I will not use intoxicating liquors as a beverage'*. Lectures were often illustrated by magic lanterns (the 'Power Point' of yesteryear), and noted personalities of the day were invited to speak. For the deprived children of Stepney, who witnessed daily the impact of alcohol on their fathers—and often their mothers—the movement gave hope. And how exciting it was to watch a magic lantern show!

During the long summer school holidays and lighter evenings, with increased time to play outside, the roads would be re-laid in hot, black, sticky tar! Rosie would hear the shrieks of the mothers as their children came home for tea with tar stuck to their clothes, their hands, and especially their knees. There were likely many boxed ears during those weeks. The return to school, and minor respite for mothers, marked the onset of autumn—shortened days and early evenings, with beautiful overlapping tones of brown, orange, red and gold.

Lily Eleanor and the family had their seasonal routines and would pack away summer clothes at the start of winter, keeping the garments fresh and clean. Winter clothes were cleaned and packed away at the end of March and swapped for lighter summer clothes with some knitwear (all hand-knitted) kept back for spring coolness. Lily Eleanor dressed smartly and took pride in her children's appearance. She wore long skirts and cotton blouses with high necks. She liked to colour match a jacket to a skirt; lighter colours during the week, but on Sundays, she would wear a brown skirt and colour-matched jacket. She never went out without a hat. There was a local market where a lady sold handmade hats and she would take Rosie as a treat, and they would try on all the hats.

Lily Eleanor was very protective of her children. Although she could not express emotion towards them, she was ceaseless in her worry about them. Rosie was developing into a tomboy. She loved to be outside and up The Waste, running free and wild. But her mother only agreed if she was with a crowd of children and if she took Ted with her. The first caveat was easy. The second was restrictive. Rosie could never go anywhere without Ted tagging along or being told by her mother to look after him. Occasionally, Rosie did complain.

"I am fed up with this," she would say to Lily Eleanor.

"Just you look after him," was her mother's succinct reply.

Her mother's instructions were never contradicted. And Ted did need looking after. He was not a robust child. Not sickly, just small and a bit fragile. As soon as school was over—and the hours were long, 8:30 a.m. to 4 or 4:30 p.m.—the children would gather like a migrating herd and go up The Waste. There was always a baby in a pram (the sibling being told to walk the baby) and as the herd walked and bayed, more children would say,

"Where are you going?" and join the swell. Rosie loved to join in all the games, frequently falling over and scraping her knees or being pushed over—albeit playfully. Looking out for Ted was a burden for a happy-go-lucky tomboy, but she took her responsibilities seriously, and he certainly had less scraped knees. He would join in with the children creating make-shift homes, welcoming visitors with grand gestures, and soothing the crying baby doll. Rosie shuddered at the thought of him playing a swashbuckling pirate with a sword. However innocent the game started, it always progressed to unbridled energy with abundant chasing and extensive falling. On one occasion, Rosie did have to visit the doctor with a badly cut knee and retained the scar. But 'cry-babies' were shunned at home and she learned to be stoic from a young age. A visit to the doctor cost sixpence, so it had to be serious to go. For any cut or sore, you came away with a purple ointment, and it seemed to do the job of healing. No one complained or took time off from school.

Lily Eleanor was also terrified of her children (especially the girls) being plucked from the street by slave traders. Living so near to the docks and being married to a sailor who had travelled the world, and loved a good yarn (nautical slang for a tale of dubious exploits), she heard such dreadful stories—whether myth or not—of fiendish gangs of eight scouring the streets for stray innocent children. Like a giant spider weaving an invisible, enveloping net in which to hook their prey, they would whisk the innocents swiftly away to their waiting ships before disappearing over the horizon.

In the early 1900s, few residents of the East End of London had met people from exotic faraway lands. There was a growing Chinese population, but seeing other exotic people was rare. Thus, when a tall, lean but muscular man with glowing bronzed skin and a shock of wild dark hair, dressed in a black suit and carrying a suitcase knocked at their door in Gold Street in the early 1920s, Lily Eleanor (whose community majored in short, ashen-faced, mousy-haired inhabitants), panicked and hid in the cupboard under the stairs with Rosie and Ted. She was paralysed with fear and hid for nearly twenty minutes before venturing out. She later found out that the visitor was a hawker off a recently docked ship and was trying to sell his wares door-to-door from his suitcase. That explanation did not allay her fears.

9

Lily Eleanor had an ulterior motive for her insistence that Rosie took responsibility for Ted: in the years before Rosie was born, and when Lily Blanche was with her granny, she had volunteered at The Christ Church in Jamaica Street (just around the corner) and at the almshouses in the Mile End Road. The 'Trinity Green Almshouses' and its Chapel were built in 1695 to provide housing for, quote: *'28 decay'd Masters & Commanders of Ships or ye Widows of such'*, end quote. The almshouses were arranged in two rows, facing a central green and a chapel. In 1895, the almshouses were threatened with closure but they were saved by a public campaign led by Charles Robert Ashbee and were the first buildings to be put on his 'Preservation Register' (as Grade 1 Listed Buildings), which many years later became the listed building system. Their history includes a connection with William Booth, who founded the Salvation Army. He preached in the Vine Tavern in front of the almshouses, and in 1927, a bronze bust was installed at the almshouses in his honour. Lily Eleanor and the Vicar of The Christ Church attended the ceremony, although Lily Eleanor didn't care much for the history—it was the community involvement that ensured her presence. Rosie, however, lapped up the history (gleaned from the Vicar) and would daydream about the '*decay'd*' officers of the sea sitting and puffing pipes in their tiny homes, recounting their shanty tales to anyone who visited and always having a tot of rum to offer. Her young mind took the positive path and not that of poverty, poor health, and the certainty that death was getting closer. Lily Eleanor took all that in her stride.

As Rosie was a good girl who valued family, her mother knew she could trust her to look out for Ted after school, thus enabling Lily Eleanor to revitalise her community work. Released from the shackles of family life (and with an absent husband), Lily Eleanor was driven to help her community and thus felt validated by her contribution to those more in need. She could not see the irony that her husband felt, and was doing the same, albeit in a commercial environment. Neither validated the other in their marriage partnership—their true selves only thrived when away from each other, and the marital home.

Rosie was blossoming. She was bright, energetic and eager to learn and explore. Her mother taught her to knit, but not to cook—that was not Lily Eleanor's greatest skill, or interest. Staple stews with lots of vegetables, sweet rice puddings and eggs with bread or toast were the mainstays of the weekly menus; but there was always an abundance of fresh fruit that would spill over the edges of the glass fruit bowl, whilst large sunshine yellow bananas perched precariously on the top. Rosie drew and practised her reading and writing, and at age seven, her mother paid for her to begin piano lessons with her aunt. Rosie didn't have to be urged; she flew into Granny's house at the allotted times, like a bee desperate for a nectar fix, and immersed herself into a world of music—the piano lessons always seemed too short. The upright piano in the front parlour at home came to life as her long, slender fingers glided along the keys and reflected in the garnet shellac while she took heed of everything her aunt had said. She practised regularly at home, and in winter (in the unheated parlour) would shrug off the cold damp air that hung from the high ceiling and dribbled like a huge invisible dewlap around her as she embraced her evolving world. As her technique and the seasons improved, the vibrant sounds resonating throughout the otherwise sombre room cheered the atmosphere, and even the goldfish developed a healthy sheen as the rhythms gently swished its water.

Rosie began to spend more time at Granny's and experienced some jealousy for the first time in her young life: she discovered that her sister was firmly embedded as a favourite, something that Rosie had not witnessed before. She knew that Lily Blanche was not as robust as her, but Rosie's thoughts would turn to wondering why she, Rosie, had to look out for Ted, had to help with chores around the house, and had to go to the markets with her mother, whilst her sister did not have any responsibilities. However, from a young age, Rosie was in awe of her granny and loved to stand on the sidelines and absorb the atmosphere of a home that was run so differently from her own.

She was dispatched on Sundays to run errands for Granny, who would be dressed in her full white chef's uniform, including the toque blanche (hat), creating and cooking the family meals. Elizabeth Emily had rules about Sundays: you could cook to feed the family and play music, but you could not knit or play cards.

Only the Jewish-owned shops opened on a Sunday. Gold Street had a line of terraced houses on one side where many Russian Jews had settled. Rosie found her neighbours good, kind, generous and industrious. Their business acumen supported the community with premises making beautiful clothes for all the family, jewellers, bakeries, and grocery shops.

The Jewish residents were proud of their faith and adhered to the Sabbath rules, quote, *to do no manner of work,* end quote. As the Jewish Sabbath ran from Friday evening to Saturday evening, their shops would open again on a Sunday. Rosie was happy to be welcomed into their houses during the Sabbath to light the fires and take their cakes to a baker who would cook them in their ovens. She would be given little tokens, like some 'matzah' (unleavened bread). There was an enhanced sense of community and everyone helped each other. If there was a Jewish wedding, it was a big event and everyone was invited to the celebrations, regardless of faith.

Rosie would be given a shopping list at Granny's and, on her return, she would watch Granny prepare, create and bake: aromatic fish in pastry, meat pies and puddings, apple tarts, sponge cakes and more. No ingredient was ever weighed. Granny had one of the first electric cookers. It covered half a wall and had an ominous, big red emergency light. Rosie was terrified of it.

Granny's Sunday teas were legendary, but you had to receive a formal invitation. A lavish spread would greet the guests in the front parlour, an array of cakes was displayed on the upright piano, and a large table, covered with a crisp linen tablecloth, displayed the mouth-watering food in tureens with ornate servers, with tableware and cutlery lying proudly alongside. Rosie experienced such a spread in late 1929 when her Uncle Wilfred (Wilf) remarried. Wilfred Arthur was Edmund's third brother, born in 1894, and he lived close by. Wilf was a tailor's cutter but went to sea during World War I, joining up in January 1916 and completing three years. Wilf was taller than Edmund at 5'8½" tall, with dark brown hair and a fresh complexion. Before he joined up, he already had a butterfly tattooed on his right forearm and 'Lizzie' tattooed on his left forearm. He was a 'bit of a lad' and Rosie liked him, but she wasn't confident enough in company to ask him who 'Lizzie' was, so she created a little story that Lizzie was his first true love, but that the love was unrequited and he had to live with her name etched into his flesh for eternity, relentlessly tearing at his heart. This story satisfied her enquiring mind. His first wife died young in 1926 and he remarried in 1929, with his mother putting on a grand spread in celebration, which included big tins of 'Sailor Slice' Fine Salmon, which at that time was somewhat of a luxury. Rosie absorbed the etiquette of eating in a semi-formal environment, together with good manners when in company and enjoying the conversations of her close relatives. Over time, she knew more about her father's family than she did about her own mother and father.

10

Rosie never understood her mother's compunction to help at the church so often. She was not religious and never attended services but helped with the money-raising events, such as jumble sales, and celebrations such as Easter and the harvest festival when the church would be adorned. Rosie, however, was sent to church three times on a Sunday: morning service, Sunday school in the afternoon and the 6:00 p.m. service. She hated the morning service as the sermons were all 'fire, brimstone, and damnation'. She was also sent to the Band of Hope meetings, even though her father and maternal grandparents ran a pub. Rosie signed the Band of Hope pledge and would live by it for the whole of her life. It is likely that Rosie was singled out for a strong Christian upbringing to appease the vicar, who must have mused over why Lily Eleanor did not attend church services. But he valued her help and her loyalty. Lily Eleanor supported the vicar in whatever he asked and visited the needy. Rosie found it hard to feign a community spirit and compassion, when at Christmas, Lily Eleanor would bring home umpteen turkeys to be plucked and prepared for the oven, but for other people. It was Rosie's job to clear up the thick carpet of bronze feathers from the kitchen table and floor, and rogue feathers would float in the warm kitchen air for several days, like butterflies abandoning pollination to rest in the warm, buoyant breeze.

Rosie knew the vicar from attending services and the Band of Hope, and she was invited to play the piano at Sunday school. She found fulfilment and joy in the young children singing hymns and carols to her music. The vicar had a car and would occasionally take Lily Eleanor, Rosie and Ted out for a treat. One such treat was a lengthy trip to the watercress farms in Berkshire—it took a couple of hours to get there—and a trip to a plant nursery, where Rosie saw a huge field of gladioli, the strong thrusting stems ablaze with a rainbow of colours. This would be the embryo of Rosie's lifelong love of gladioli. The children enjoyed the car ride itself, feeling very grand as they were chauffeured around the countryside, playing 'I Spy' and singing ditties.

No one went on holiday in those days. Some folk went hop picking in Kent, including a neighbour of Rosie's, and came back with lively tales. But Lily Eleanor was not interested. Sleeping in dusty barns after a hard day handpicking hops, cooking kippers on a bonfire, and enduring rudimental hygiene facilities were not for her. The church organised holidays in the country for the children. The offers came mostly from farmers who would welcome a couple of children for a week, or perhaps two, *to enjoy the health benefits of the countryside*. Rosie was sent once and returned after a week, tired and confused. Some of the farmers used the arrangements as free labour, making the children work all day without providing adequate food and with very basic facilities. Lily Eleanor was forthright to the vicar in her condemnation of the arrangements.

11

School days were happy, fulfilling times for Rosie. She was bright, attentive, and creative, and she craved to develop outside of her home. From the Baker Street nursery school, she progressed to Red Coats Christian Primary School. The school had existed since 1714, in various guises, starting as a voluntary subscription school for the clothing and education of a limited number of boys born within Mile End Old Town. She did not have to wear a uniform, but on special occasions and celebrations, one girl and one boy would dress in the old-style historical clothing. The teachers and head were all female, and the schooling was strict, but Rosie thrived in an environment that enabled her to learn without distractions. They performed a Nativity Play each Christmas and, as Rosie had short hair, she always played the King, sporting a cape and a cardboard crown. Their Nativity Play was so polished they were invited to other schools to perform.

Rosie learned to swim at primary school. The pupils marched in an orderly, if slightly swaying, crocodile line, with cloth bags containing a costume and a towel, with the string-pull closure swung over a shoulder, chattering nineteen-to-a dozen to 'The People's Palace' in the Mile End Road. Rosie was proud to gain her 10-yard swimming certificate.

The People's Palace was an innovation in recreation and education. The overall scheme covered five acres of land. The central 'Queen's Hall' was opened by Queen Victoria on the 14th of May, 1887, with work in the following October on the classrooms, exhibition hall, swimming baths, and gymnasium. The development was completed in 1892.

The Queen's Hall was a grand building with stained glass windows and a vaulted ceiling. There was a rostrum at one end with a handsome organ provided by a private donor at a cost of £10,000. In 1887, that was a fortune. The hall was abuzz with music recitals during the week and, on Sundays, sacred music was played. Sir Edmund Hay Currie, the driving force behind the development, believed that the warm, welcoming, well-lit hall, with its beauty and music, would tempt people away from the pubs and be a catalyst for change.

An eight-sided free library with a reading room was opened behind The Queen's Hall in June 1888. The shelves held 250,000 books which were all donated by publishers and authors, and nearly all of the periodicals and magazines available were provided for free. Estimates at the time put visitor numbers at 900 to 1100 each weekday. Behind The Queen's Hall was a glass-covered winter garden with tropical palms, flowers and fruits, creating an exotic, multi-coloured world within—so far removed from the functional environment of London's East End. The Victorians were avid in their desire to know more about the worlds outside of their own, and they did it in style: immersed for a few hours in a fantastical garden that belied the grey skies, rain and mist of the true surroundings, a person would be rejuvenated in both body and spirit.

A technical college developed from the schools that were built within the project, with day and evening classes that were open to women; an innovation itself. A comprehensive prospectus included tailoring, carpentry, photography, needlework, book-keeping and French. It is recorded that in 1890, 5500 students attended classes. People desired to better themselves, to learn new skills and inject knowledge and passion into their conversations and debates with family and friends. The Queen's Hall survived World War I, but tragically, would be completely destroyed by fire in 1931 (when Rosie was only eleven years old). It was never rebuilt. The site would be redeveloped but with an emphasis on education only. It would become 'The Queen Mary's College' in December 1934. Rosie would enjoy her visits to the swimming pool but would never get the chance to gaze in awe at the magnificence of The Queen's Hall, hear the music, or dance. She didn't feel a great sense of loss that an alcohol-free haven of social interaction, with beautiful music, and the chance to dance was denied to her—she did not miss what she did not have—but it was lost forever, together with Sir Edmund Hay Currie's spectacular ambition.

12

As Rosie grew, she explored the immediate locality and knew all the families. The shops so close to hand were taken for granted. Here are the records of 1921 for Gold Street, citing the building numbers:

113	Mrs Fanny Joseph, Fancy Draper
115	Isaac Mautner, Provision Dealer
117	Joseph Harris, Butcher
119	Abraham Rosienfield, Chandlers Shop
121	Davis Walters, Tailor
125	Barnett Kopinsky, Tobacconist
127	Lewis Silverman, China Dealer
129	Harry Atkins, Greengrocer
135	Kloegman & Co, Blouse Makers

137   Israel Bernstein, Bootmaker
141   Edward Lovett, Coal Dealer
South Side
40   Abraham Spielsinger, Proprietor, Crown Hall
42   Geo Sully & Co, Whalebone Manufacturers
50   Aaron Cohen, Barrow Lender
80   Henry Ellison, Ladies' Tailor

In the interlocking streets are listed: Fishmongers, Laundry, Hairdressers, Corset Makers, Stationers, Haberdashers, Embroiderer, Dyer and Cleaner, Wheelwright, Umbrella Maker, Bakers, Beer Retailers, Confectioners, Artificial Teeth Maker, and a Milliner. There were a couple of shops that Rosie visited daily: Robins Corner Shop was run by a couple with two daughters and had everyday stock cupboard items (non-perishables) and especially biscuits. They came in tins and you could buy a pennyworth of broken biscuits. This was a really cheap treat as the Robins would pick out the nice ones for the children. Rosie's favourite was a melt-in-the-mouth Italian wafer. When you went into Robins, there was always something tempting on the counter, perhaps honeycomb or toffees. The owners also ran a savings scheme. Lily Eleanor would have a savings card and send Rosie each week with a halfpenny, and then at Christmas they would collect a big variety tin of sweets, which included jellies with a sweet liquid centre—absolute bliss for the children. Robins had many sweet treats that children could buy for only a farthing, making the shop very popular.

Milk was delivered. Rosie would take a jug out and it would be filled for two and a half pennies a pint, but you could also top up at the dairy. When it was hot, the children would run behind the ice cart that carried the fresh milk, pleading for a chunk of ice. Alice's Dairy was on the opposite corner to Robins. Rosie loved going into the dairy. It was so cool and clean and smelled delicious. It had a shiny marble floor that looked almost wet with its high gloss, and the milk, cheese and butter were cooled with ice, which chinked as the produce was lifted for purchase, causing the chunks to gently fall back and regroup.

There were several local markets, but the biggest was Chrisp Street in Poplar, which involved a tram ride and great excitement for Rosie. They sold absolutely everything. There were shops and stalls out in the open, and shopkeepers would stand outside their shops, touting for business and competing with the animated invitations from the stall holders. The produce was fresh and unprocessed. Bananas were sold from the backs of lorries—direct from the docks on huge bunches—with their stems intact. The stallholders would just pull off what you wanted. Tomatoes were loose and popped into your bag. If you bought potatoes, you were given a bunch of mint and 'pot herbs' such as onions and carrots were just thrown into your open bag, free of charge. Nothing was weighed. Sugar came in a blue bag and was tuppence farthing, and tea came in penny packets. No branding, just plain packaging. Newly laid eggs were 1½ pennies each and had a deep golden yolk.

Rosie revered the fish—particularly smoked haddock—and the abundant seafood. She loved winkles and had mastered skewering the worm-like organisms out of their shells with a pin, dipping them into some vinegar and popping them, with relish, into her mouth before swallowing them whole. On these visits, they would have smoked haddock for tea, and Rosie couldn't wait for the hot, chubby, amber flesh to be tipped out of the pan, topped with a dollop of butter that she could watch sliding slowly down the sides, before mixing with the juice poured from the poaching pan to create a creamy golden gravy. Rosie's mouth would be salivating as she performed her ritual of dipping a chunk of crusty bread into the gravy—savouring its distinctive taste—before tearing at the flesh with a fork. Rosie adored that market day and could put aside her frustration at having to accompany her mother everywhere.

13

Noises that invade and attack your senses, smells that both delight and disgust and scenes that excite: Salmon Lane market was abuzz. Whether the sky was blue or grey, the climate hot or cold, shopkeepers and stall holders held their potential customers in rapture. This was another occasion when Rosie was happy to accompany her mother.

Lily Eleanor sometimes travelled further afield to Salmon Lane in Limehouse for a Saturday market. A cornucopia of shops including butchers, grocers, dressmakers, shoe makers, drapers and chemists, with shopkeepers standing in pole position at their frontage, denigrating the wares of the stall holders against their own, and poised like big cats to pounce, coax and corral customers through their door.

"Fresh rabbits, the best in London, only a shilling!" vying with,

"Get your rabbits here, darlings, chubby and fresh, ripe for the pot, and I'll throw in your onions and carrots."

The Regent's Canal Dock was close to the southern end of Salmon Lane and cargo was unloaded from merchant ships and transferred to canal narrowboats, providing a steady stream of fresh produce for the businesses. The rivalry between shopkeeper and stall holder was tangible but part of the experience, together with the colourful language and the backdrop of rousing organ music. This was not a gentle Saturday morning stroll to the shops. This market was a lifeline for those whose existence depended on getting adequate food and clothing for the little money they had.

The market was packed from end to end with buyers ducking to miss the freshly killed rabbits hanging on the butcher's stalls and keeping their purses and wallets close to their bodies to foil the pickpockets.

Lily Eleanor was a seasoned shopper and made her way deftly through the crowds to each stall, opening her bag for vegetables to be tossed in and picking the chubbiest of the rabbits. Freshness was never an issue. She preferred shops for clothing, and the drapers was Rosie's favourite. The assistants were so helpful, going time and time again to the tall wooden racks of drawers and identifying contents on the front and their sizes. Open a polished drawer front and ladies' vests and knickers were so neatly folded it was a shame to disturb them. Shopping done and new underwear neatly parcelled in brown paper and safe in Rosie's hands, Lily Eleanor would leave her in the safety of the shop for a few minutes, sitting her (with agreement from the assistants) quietly in the corner. Rosie did not know at first, but this disappearing act was to visit a 'bookie' in the market and place a bet on the horses. This was unusual practice for a woman of Lily Eleanor's standing. But who could deny her the adrenaline rush of placing, and perhaps winning, a bet? Besides, the bookie did not mind who placed the bet. When Rosie found out, she wondered what the vicar would have thought! Lily Eleanor was wise to dabble away from her doorstep.

And then there was Wickhams. In the Mile End Road, there was a parade of shops, but with so many shops near to home, and the markets, Lily Eleanor only made the trip for something she could not get locally. But then the Wickhams Department Store's *grand scheme* came to fruition. In planning for many years, Wickhams wanted to rival the West End department stores and, in particular, upstage Selfridges. The Wickham family were drapers and had three shops at numbers 69, 71 and 73 Mile End Road. A family business of clockmakers and jewellers occupied number 75 and, as the Wickhams thrived, they agreed, in 1892, to move to number 81 and let Wickhams expand into no 75.

The impetus did not waver for a further thirty-five years, and gradually the Wickham family acquired the whole block of shops in the parade—except number 81—and plans were finally progressed for the major refurbishment. They assumed that the jeweller would sell, but the family business at number 81 refused to move out of their premises at any price: number 81 was their history, with many of the family being born there, and with a solid, profitable business, nothing was going to move them out. The standoff was never resolved. However, there was a minor compromise, and the jewellers sold their back garden to Wickhams who then went ahead with their plans, building around and behind the jewellers, and both continued to trade.

When the scheme was completed in 1927, the shoppers flocked to Wickhams, despite the building being rather odd: with elegant edifices positioned on either side of number 81, the small independent shop. An iconic clock tower was the crowning glory and believing the jewellers would eventually sell, the column to the right was built with a flat side so that the two split buildings could be seamlessly joined in the future. The jewellers did not falter in their resolve not to sell, and the business (and building) was passed down through the family, firmly ensconced, like a truculent child refusing to acknowledge any wrongdoing, and mouthing a silent "Got you!" each time the door opened and closed.

Lily Eleanor would make an occasional trip to the *Wonder of Wickhams,* and Rosie would glow with anticipation. Used to independent shops selling specific products, here was everything under one roof; a labyrinth of rooms, corridors and counters with clothes, furniture, household items (especially kitchen gadgets and utensils)—and shortly after opening—electrical items. You could get your hair cut and styled, and they offered credit, called 'tick' and had their own 'tally men' who went door to door, collecting the dues. Folk could improve their homes and lives without ready cash, and it was contagious: touch something, and you were compelled to buy it. At Christmas, the store could match Santa's Workshop at the North Pole; the decorations and sheer scale of choice sent Lily Eleanor and Rosie's senses reeling.

It was an integral part of Rosie's life as she grew, but, although it would survive the London Blitz (in 1940), the allure of the independent department store faded in the 1960s, and Wickhams sold up and moved out, leaving number 81 intact.

14

Shouts of laughter, the thwap of a skipping rope on the pavement, and the rhythmic yet gentle thud of feet vying to win at hopscotch competed with the rousing calls of the hawkers, plying their wares from a horse and cart or hand barrow. The children playing outdoors in Gold Street would giggle and nudge each other as Mr. Henry Martin, from number 33, would amble pass them declaring, "I'm just going on my trek."

They all knew what this meant: down to the pub on the corner for a pint of beer and then back up the road to number 33. This trek was undertaken several times a day. Mr. Martin worked at the docks, but daily work was not guaranteed; you could turn up for your shift and be sent home. It was a difficult life, not knowing what a new sunrise would bring. How could the Band of Hope persuade hard working men like Mr. Martin that his life would be better without his pints of beer? What was the alternative respite from the daily grind?

The hawkers aroused great excitement in the children. The Italians came with their gorgeous ice cream in barrels and peanuts were roasted nearby in the Mile End Road and brought round the streets with roasted chestnuts. Sunday brought the Muffin Man and a horse and cart with cockles and mussels, shrimps, celery, and other delicious Sunday tea goodies. The children would crowd the carts, imbibing the smells and praying their parents had a few pennies left to appease their rumbling tummies.

It was vital to have a cat—not as a pet, but as a mouser—and Lily Eleanor always had one. You paid a halfpenny a day and a fresh lump of cat food on a stick of wood was secured under the brass door knocker—high enough to stop passing animals from stealing a treat. Everything that was needed to sustain life was within a mile or two of their home, and community and belonging was provided by friends and neighbours just outside the front door.

People did not travel far from their own communities, except on special occasions. The British Queen pub was two tram rides away from Gold Street, so Lily Eleanor did not routinely visit her parents, and Rosie had only minor contact with her Aunt Bessie, who did not come to Gold Street for any occasion. The family did visit the pub in Shoreditch each Easter and Christmas. The pub was cavernous with large rooms above, and they would stay overnight. For Rosie and her siblings, it was an adventure akin to going on holiday, and Rosie and Ted could explore the pub with impunity and play hide and seek in the immense cellar. It was a duty for Lily Eleanor that she was obliged to undertake, and although Eva (the cleaner) kept her distance from Edmund during these visits, Lily Eleanor detected an unusual interest from Edmund in Eva's cleaning duties.

Sarah and Robert did visit their daughter once a week: on a Wednesday evening when they went to the Stratford Empire for a variety show and always came to visit before the show. When Rosie and Ted came home from school, everything had to be immaculate in the house, and she never understood why. Her grandparents were not posh or snobby, but definitely genteel. Robert was very smart, with an overcoat and a cap, and Sarah was always in black velvet, like Queen Victoria, with a cape and bonnet. Violets were her favourite flower, and she always wore a corsage of violets. They would walk from the tram stop, arm in arm, slowly navigating the hazards of the time: horse manure in the roads, streets full of exuberant children playing noisy games and puddles of murky black coal dust if there had been rain. They had a regal air. Robert was generous and would give the urchins in the street a penny, and a florin (two shillings or twenty-four pennies) to each of his grandchildren. The children looked forward to their visits, even if they had to be clean and tidy and on best behaviour—twenty-four pennies bought a lot of joy.

Robert was particularly generous at Christmas. Unpretentious as well as kind, he would leave an envelope on the mantelpiece containing money to buy the three grandchildren a new outfit for the coming year. Each outfit would be handmade by the Jewish tailors. It would be skirts and blouses for the girls and a jacket and short trousers for Ted, the only son. Robert also put money directly into their palms, gently squeezing them shut as he put in a florin or perhaps a half-crown, whilst putting a finger to his lips in an exaggerated manner and whispering, "Hush!"

Lily Eleanor had inherited her father's generosity, but Rosie did not witness any real emotion between him and Sarah, or between Lily Eleanor and her mother. Lily Eleanor did not look forward to the visits and feared her mother's disapproval (a by-product of her childhood). Sarah was emotionally cold, with little conversation and scant intent to offer praise or encouragement.

15

One of the close neighbours (the Bakers) had a large family of nine children—five girls and four boys. Mrs Baker had a difficult life with a husband who liked his drink and didn't always have work, leaving her to take care of their large, needy family. She wasn't much of a cook, or housekeeper, and struggled to keep everything together, evocative of the nursery rhyme *'there was an old lady who lived in a shoe; she had so many children she didn't know what to do'*. She had a gas stove but would cook herrings by putting them directly on the gas ring. With only fundamental cooking abilities, the household menu was somewhat predictable and included a substantial amount of 'stale bread', obtained cheaply when the bakery was about to close each day. Three of the girls worked at a local brewery washing glass bottles, and their hands would be red, raw, and often bleeding. The brewery did not provide protective gloves, and Mrs. Baker could not afford soothing balm. Her daughters dreamed of marrying and escaping. Another daughter, Maudie, was the same age as Rosie, and she worked in a factory sticking labels on tins; she developed an allergic skin reaction to the glue, but, in the absence of other work, she had to carry on.

Lily Eleanor had sympathy for the family and was persuaded to sublet the large room upstairs to a newly married daughter, Annie. She had married an Irish chap named Wogan who drove a horse and cart and delivered industrial coal. He would often come home during his shift and dump huge lumps of coal in the road for their fire—huge because it was not domestic coal. Too soon it became clear that Annie was lazy and not house-proud. They produced three children in quick succession, and the five of them were living, eating, washing and sleeping in one room. Chamber pots were a necessity during the evening and night since using the toilet involved a long walk outside, in the dark, whatever the weather. The gas cooker on the landing was used extensively. However, her repertoire was limited, and the whole house reeked of cabbage and greens being boiled for too long. At least she used a saucepan. The air was permeated with unpleasant, often unhealthy smells, and a lot of noise. Lily Eleanor could not evict them due to a sense of community, and they always paid the rent, but there were occasions when she would storm out the kitchen, call up the stairs, "Keep the noise down, up there!" and mutter under her breath how she had made a big mistake when she sublet the room to them. When Rosie went to the top of the house to run errands for Mrs. Lefly, she would race up the stairs holding her breath as she passed the large pail full of soiled nappies on their way to the washhouse.

With her work in the community, Lily Eleanor met a lot of people in need, and the loan of an odd sixpence developed into a community service, the details of which she recorded in her head, with ready cash carried in a money belt under her clothes, and never removed. Rosie knew that people came to her mother for small loans, but it was never discussed. It was the time of the 'Great Depression' [1929] with devastating unemployment, but men still spent in the public houses— their only source of respite— and the women were expected to manage. There was often a knock at the door from a neighbour asking to borrow a penny or a sixpence. Sixpence (a 'tanner') could buy a lot of food.

If the rent was not paid, eviction followed fast. Mrs. Baker was always in debt, and Lily Eleanor was constantly lending her pennies and tanners. She would come for a 'penny for the gas', which gave a lot of gas; the supply did not shut off suddenly—it would go low first to give more time to put money back into the meter. Lily Eleanor could not turn her back on genuine need. Rosie would hear Mrs. Baker tapping on the window, and Lily Eleanor would say, "Go away, woman, you owe me enough already."

But she would always relent and lend her a tanner. She knew that she was privileged to have a husband in work, and she lent money to support her neighbours, not for personal gain. People honoured their debts, but not always with speed. This community service, however, snowballed as word spread, and developed beyond close neighbours to the community as a whole. And as the requested loans grew bigger, Lily Eleanor added a small amount of interest. Whenever Rosie and her mother were out and about, Lily Eleanor would say, "Wait there, I will just be a minute," as she dropped into someone's house.

Memories of war had faded but were supplanted by the intense reality of survival, and Lily Eleanor had become a money lender.

16

As Ted grew, his confidence improved and he did go out on his own occasionally, but this did not always instil confidence in his family. He would go down to the docks, and because he was small and white-blonde, he was a favourite with the dockers and they looked out for him, making sure he was safe and did not go anywhere dangerous. Ted loved it. They would share their sandwiches with him and give him a banana to take home. Only on this particular day, he came home not with a banana but with a large, colourful parrot in a cage, straight off a ship and almost as big as him. Edmund was home that evening and was not best pleased.

"What the dickens have you got there?" he said, as his face grew darker.

"A man gave me this to take home," said Ted, with a smidgeon of pride.

Importing parrots was restricted, and Edmund could have been heavily fined.

"You must NEVER take presents from strangers. Put the cage down and go to your room. NOW!"

With trembling lips, tears welling in his eyes and a crestfallen stance, Ted disappeared through the kitchen door while Edmund took the parrot straight back to the docks and gave the dockers a piece of his mind.

At eleven years of age (1931), Rosie won a scholarship to the senior school, Green Coats School, or as it was formally named, 'the Hamlet of Ratcliffe School'. Still in Stepney and walking distance from home, this school did have a uniform, and Lily Eleanor took Rosie to get it, at quite a cost. There was a green pleated tunic, cream-coloured blouses, a yellow tie, black stockings and black lace-up shoes. This was the first time that Rosie wore shoes and not boots. In those days, in the East End of London, shoes were for the affluent who did not routinely have to navigate the grimy streets and walk everywhere, whatever the weather. In the summer, a blazer was worn with a Panama hat, and in the winter, a raincoat with a black hat. The hats were banded in green and yellow. Lily Eleanor and Edmund were forward thinking in their approach to education for Rosie, even though she was a girl and expected to marry and not forge a career.

At senior school she studied English, maths, algebra, sciences and French. There were mixed classes and mixed teachers. The male teachers, called masters, taught Rosie in science, and in shorthand and typing. Typewriting was taught blind with the keys covered. Rosie was a natural typist and, in 1936, would get a distinction in both shorthand and typing exams adjudicated by The London Chamber of Commerce.

Rosie was athletic and enjoyed the sports classes, which a female teacher led, and the girls wore shorts and dark green knickers. Sports involved a lot of jumping, skipping, barre work and running on the field tracks. (The swimming lessons had stopped after leaving primary school). There was a big sports day in Leytonstone each year with a lot of running races, and Rosie embraced the team spirit, cheering on friends and classmates.

Her Aunt Elsie had learned to play the accordion and, after a regular piano lesson, she played for Rosie, and Rosie was smitten. It was further stimulation to her intellect, and she absorbed new challenges like a living sponge. Rosie adored her aunt's beautiful black and gold accordion and mused that it had belonged to a royal family somewhere. Its ornate gold piping glinted as it caught the light when the bellows breathed in and out. It seemed to Rosie that the instrument had life.

Lily Eleanor agreed that Rosie could take accordion lessons. They were two shillings for each lesson. She was taught by a local young man and was taken to a big music shop in Aldgate, where an accordion was bought that fitted snugly in a lined container that resembled a case that would house a large, old-style typewriter. It cost £12. By the age of fifteen, Rosie was proficient and ached to get home and feel her fingers stretch on the keys as she coaxed the bellows to bring her instrument to life. She felt the first stirring of adulthood and would stand in front of a mirror whilst she played and, sometimes, did not recognise the poised, confident woman she was becoming. But she was still a schoolgirl and when she was asked to play at her school, the headmaster said, with a wink, "That is a very nice typewriter!" Rosie reddened a little and giggled.

Rosie, aged fifteen years (1935)

Rosie was a capable artist, good at crafts, and she could sing. Free of the modern-day obsessions of television, computers and mobile phones, Rosie's evenings were a healthy mix of play, music practice, knitting, reading, and helping Lily Eleanor. She had her daily chores: polishing the brass door knocker and cleaning and buffing the front step. But it was the washing of the huge net curtains that tested her compliance. She would come home from school, and Lily Eleanor would light the copper in the washhouse. When the water was warm, the nets would be draped on top and carefully pushed in with wooden tongs, then gently swirled. After rinsing, squeezing, and folding, Rosie would turn the handle of the big mangle whilst her mother slowly fed in the mound of delicate material as if through a conveyor belt. Meticulously folded between them, Rosie would be dispatched to the far end of the backyard, and with the nets stretching back to her mother (and afraid that her arms would give), they would hang them on the triple, side by side, washing lines. Woe betides if they touched the ground!

17

Rosie started her period at age thirteen. Her mother was matter of fact about it, and Rosie was not close to her sister, but she could talk to close girlfriends and did not find her situation challenging. Like her mother before her, she was given rags and a belt that held the rags in place. Used rags were either boiled in the big copper, or burnt on the fire in the kitchen, which was always ablaze. All waste was burnt on the fire. There was minimal packaging, and food waste was limited.

The leaving age for senior school was at fourteen years. However, Rosie was picked for the shorthand/typewriting course, which meant she stayed on until she was sixteen. This dovetailed with Ted as he was not academic, being much better with his hands, and they would leave school at the same time. Ted would later secure a daytime apprenticeship making lenses for spectacles and thrive in his career.

While Rosie and Ted were at school, Lily Eleanor immersed herself in more community work, and the children soon became 'latch key' kids. She was rarely at home when the children returned from school, being either at The Christ Church in Jamaica Street or the almshouses in the Mile End Road, where she looked after two old ladies. With the exception of Thursdays, the family meals around the kitchen fire waned, and too often Rosie would find a note on the table with some coppers (slang for pennies) when she got home from school. The note would instruct Rosie to take Ted to the Pie and Mash Shop to buy their supper. Rosie liked the minced beef pie and creamy mash with the parsley sauce liquor, but Ted would pale and sway slightly when he smelt the liquor and had to stay outside the shop. The Pie and Mash shops also served eels, and the eel juice from cooking was used to make the liquor sauce. Rosie grew resentful at her mother's absence and her own increased responsibilities. Her sister did not get these responsibilities: she came home from work, went into Granny's, and would often go to a local dance. Rosie could only admire her sister's lovely dance dresses. Lily Blanche was courted and had boyfriends, some of whom were brought home. One chap was really jolly, and Rosie liked him. His family ran a big pub. But Lily Blanche fell for her Harry, who Rosie found rather moody; he never acknowledged Rosie or Ted or held any conversation with them.

Lily Blanche married Harry at The Christ Church in Jamaica Street on the 6th of June, 1937, aged twenty-two years. Her occupation on the marriage certificate confirms that she was a clerk. Rosie had no idea. She knew so little about her sister. She only knew that her sister went into London every day on the train. Harry was a porter, and at the time of the wedding, was lodging with Granny Elizabeth Emily. Rosie was asked to play the accordion at the wedding and considered this a big honour for her; and it reassured her that her sister knew something about her. The newly-weds bought their own house and chose to live in Plaistow in a 'two-up, two-down' terraced house that would only suffer minor damage during the London Blitz of 1940 and the long years of war that followed. You went from the street through the front door into the narrow lounge; a small kitchen went off to the side on the right and from there to a backyard with an outdoor toilet. At the end of the lounge was a cupboard door, and when you opened it, a set of steep stairs went up to a landing with one bedroom to the left and the second to the right. Upstairs did not have a corridor. They could have bought a brand-new house with an indoor bathroom in Chingford, outside London and in a lovely green area for less money, but Harry's sister lived in Plaistow, and he wanted to stay near his family. Community mattered.

Lily Eleanor's increasing weekday absences also meant that she was doing the family washing at night by candlelight in the outdoor washhouse, so the children were left alone again, taking themselves off to bed at the allotted time of 9 pm. Lily Eleanor could not be an affectionate mother. She was dominant and ruled the house. Her word was law. Rosie never saw her father challenge her mother, and if upset by her mother's ruling about something, she understood the futility of going to her father. Lily Eleanor supported her family in the only ways she could and was a savvy manager of the family's finances. This enabled Rosie to attend the scholarship school with a full uniform, take piano and accordion lessons, and buy an accordion. Lily Eleanor also helped her newly-wed daughter to buy a house rather than rent. But the emotional abyss would impact Rosie as it had already impacted Edmund. As for Lily Eleanor, she was content in innocent oblivion. The four seasons of life were marching on for her. Nature would not take second place. Birth, maturity, marriage and the creation of a family were already spent. She was entering her fourth season, but would it be a gentle route, through a glorious autumn of gold, copper, orange and brown or a harsh cold winter route with trees stripped of the leaves on their branches and the bark on their trunks? It was not in her hands alone.

18

It was Rosie's sixteenth year, and one that would shape her transition from schoolgirl to young woman. She had outgrown the childhood games played in the street or up The Waste, and she had been taught by her parents to play cards. She visited The Waste with girlfriends now to listen to the speakers and engage in light conversation with boys, an interest that was developing quite naturally. Indoors, she helped her mother, studied, practised her music, and was a prolific knitter. She could knit complex patterns, and they were never short of mittens, gloves, and socks. Her long, fine fingers could work their magic on any task that she undertook, expressing her creativity through deed rather than voice. Her hands glided like silk across the keyboards of her piano and accordion and guided the knitting needles without a glance. She didn't mourn the lack of conversation with her mother.

She flourished at school, where conversation and debate were unbridled and fed her enquiring mind. After school, Rosie and her school chums would go to Stepney Green, which was opposite their school. It wasn't a park as such but there were gardens and a Hall that kept horses. They liked to go and watch the horses being fed. This was a real taste of the countryside. The gardens were lovely, and they chatted and laughed as they strolled through, admiring the plants and trees, which were absent from their own streets and backyards. The girls liked to test their knowledge of nature, gleaned from lessons at school and books. They marvelled at the silver birch tree, tall and graceful with drooping branches and triangular shaped leaves, and a silvery-white bark. In autumn, they would track the leaves changing from vibrant green, to yellow and then to gold, before gently making their descent to the ground. In spring and summer, they would stand at a distance to spot the tiny birds; long-tailed tits, siskin, greenfinches, and redpolls. The birds would feed on the seeds and insects that the stately silver birch hosted. The birds may have been tiny, but their colours were grand.

Rosie loved her community. It was like being protected by a gentle force field that swirled and eddied, bubbling around the tight-knit maze of grey streets and their inhabitants. If the equilibrium was upset, the force field would gently steer her back into recovery. This proved to be vital that year when her community had an unwelcome intruder intent on causing pain and suffering. It was Sir Oswald Ernald Mosley, who brought his infamous 'Black Shirts' with him. (Mosley led a proclaimed anti-Semitic fascist movement whose uniform flaunted a black shirt to enhance their appearance of menace.)

Before Mosley appeared, the community lived in harmony and friendship, looking out for each other, and making the best of hard times. They were horrified when Mosley descended on their streets. He chose his targets carefully and always where there was a strong Jewish presence.

Mosley started holding meetings in Stepney Green because there were Jewish shops on each corner. The community felt the intimidation and witnessed the evil intent as fights broke out and blood was shed. Everyone in Rosie's world hated the Black Shirts. Mosley was a 'Sir' by virtue of his baronetcy—he was a 6th baronet—and under different circumstances, a title would have attracted respect from the community. But his sisters were pro-German and one was particularly friendly with Adolf Hitler. Mosley became an MP in 1920, first as a Conservative, then as a Labour Independent and then just Labour before he founded the 'New Party'. He lost his Smethwick (in Birmingham) seat at the 1931 General Election and in 1932, the New Party became the 'British Union of Fascists'.

Mosley secretly married his mistress in Germany at the home of Joseph Goebbels on the 6th October 1936. His new wife was Diana, one of the Mitford sisters, and Adolf Hitler was a guest of honour. Mosley spent large amounts of his personal fortune funding the British Union of Fascists.

It was a day of celebration in the East End of London when, in May 1940, Mosley (and his wife) were imprisoned. They were regarded as a threat to national security. He was released in 1943 but was politically, and irrevocably, disgraced by his association with fascism. They moved abroad in 1951 and he died in 1980.

In stark contrast, that same year, Rosie was inspired by a visit to Cunard's magnificent new ship build, *The Queen Mary*, named after the consort of King George V, Mary of Teck. Almost abandoned due to the Great Depression (a dire economic decade from 1929 to 1939 in the United Kingdom), when international passenger numbers and cargo loads fell dramatically, the keel of the ship was laid on the 31st of January, 1931, but all work stopped on the 11th of December, 1931, and the anticipated finish date of May 1932 dissipated into the ether. Simultaneously, both major shipping lines—Cunard and the White Star Line—were in trouble and appealed to the government of the day for financial help. The government was motivated to help as it was already troubled by Germany, France and Italy leading Britain in the shipping industry, and agreed to a £9.5 million loan, with the proviso that Cunard and the White Star Line merged. The decision was an easy one. Work on *The Queen Mary* restarted in March 1934, delivering a breath taking, 310-metre-long and 81,000-tons liner. It was an immediate contender for the title of the world's largest liner.

The interior fittings were styled in luscious Art Deco designs, which the public adored, and the ship gained the nickname of *The Ship of Woods*, as over fifty different woods from around the world were crafted into her design. Her maiden voyage commenced on the 27th of

May, 1936, from Southampton to New York and, although not intentionally built to challenge the transatlantic speed record, the ship was on course to be the fastest until slowed by fog in the final few days. She had sea trials from March 1936, docking in various places, and Rosie clambered on board in London, with hordes of excited viewers, and strolled along the decks and corridors (arm-in-arm with her best friend Dorothy) imbibing the opulence and grandeur whilst making teenage pacts that they would, one day, be paying passengers.

19

Rosie and Dorothy were great pals, sharing dreams, and confidences. Dorothy lived opposite The Christ Church in Jamaica Street, and her father was a local Custodian, keen to wear a uniform and not correct those who thought he was a policeman. Rosie did not warm to him. He was gruff and had two big Chow dogs that he kept in the basement and who barked aggressively at everyone. Rosie avoided going to her friend's house, so on Sundays they would go up to The Waste to listen to a speaker, plot their exciting futures, and then attend Sunday school.

When their parents allowed, they went to the local cinema, the spectacular 'Troxy'. The cinema was created by Maurice Cheepen in 1933 on the site of a demolished brewery in Stepney. It was the largest cinema in England at the time and could seat 3520. With its large sweeping staircase, chandeliers, thick carpets, and floor to ceiling mirrors in the foyer, it was indulgent. The first film to be shown there was *King Kong* in 1933 but at only thirteen, Rosie was not allowed to go that night.

Maurice Cheepen loved stunts. He would have a man dressed as a vampire handing out leaflets for *Dracula* and a horse-drawn pumpkin coach for *Cinderella*. The children were equally scared and excited! Rosie had unforgettable evenings there. Free of control and restraint, her mind soared, fantasising and diving into worlds unknown. Films had evolved from silent to 'talkies' during the late 1920s, however, an organist deftly provided additional entertainment during the screenings. Westerns with galloping horses were a favourite of the boys, who stomped their sturdy boots in time to the music, and the gallops resounded through the theatre as if a stampeding herd of cattle had escaped from the screen.

Rosie left school at sixteen and went to an employment bureau in London with her certificates and her mother. Her mother's insistence on attending was embarrassing but not up for debate. Lily Eleanor was driven to ensure that Rosie got a job in a reputable place. Was Lily Eleanor proud of her daughter's achievements at school? If she was, she did not express it. Her upbringing had impregnated her psyche as if injected with an emotion-suppressing serum. Her spirit had been crushed as a child. She was unable to fantasise, to embrace dreams and ambitions. Control was her skill: finances, the home environment, her own feelings, and control of the family. These were Lily Eleanor's expressions of love.

The employment bureau dispatched applicants for jobs immediately, and Rosie landed a job in Bread Street, near St. Paul's Cathedral, with ease. The firm was from Northern England and manufactured bed linen, but they had a small administration office in London. Rosie was soon bored. She had a lively mind and so little to do. When the office was idle, they let her knit. She had a pattern that she could do blindfolded, and she knitted multiple jumpers in her short time there. But it did not assuage her boredom. She earned nineteen shillings a week. However, this was paid by cheque, so it had to be paid into her father's bank account, which was the king's bank, Coutts. Around the same time, the bank decided to stop accepting cheques, so with this glitch, and the boredom, she returned to the employment bureau. Lily Eleanor came too, of course!

There was a vacancy at Nestlé—at the time a well-known company producing multiple milk products and chocolate—and Rosie was given a card to go there straight away as they were interviewing that day. The offices were near the Tower of London and had a huge entrance with two lifts. Rosie was impressed. Lily Eleanor did not go in but sat on a wall outside and waited. She was sure that nothing untoward would happen to Rosie inside such a building.

Rosie was greeted by a commissionaire who checked her card, confirmed that she was meeting with Mr. Perryman, and escorted her to the office. There were three girls sitting outside, so she joined them. They sat upright, like statues, hardly daring to breathe and too nervous and intimidated by their surroundings to chat to each other.

During the interview, Rosie relaxed a little and was able to talk confidently about her skills and experience. Mr. Perryman asked her to sit outside again, and she noticed that the other two girls had gone; she dared to think that the interview had gone well. She was right, and they offered her the job at £3 a week. She started in the public office, where she just did typing, but was soon moved to one of the business sections. Each section had a boss with a secretary, and Rosie joined a section that also had a young man, making four in total. Women had to leave when they got married, and three months later, when the secretary got married, Rosie was promoted.

Lily Eleanor took the whole of Rosie's wages and gave her a shilling a day. Nestlé had a lovely canteen, and lunch was only sixpence. Her fare each day was tuppence. Rosie had fourpence a day for herself. She did not expect anything else. Lily Eleanor still bought her clothes, and she had not started going to the cinema or the theatres in the West End of London. Her social life was not expensive. The lunch at Nestlé was a full meal, not a snack, and was good quality, so Rosie did not have to worry about her mother being out when she got home. She also had a 15-minute break in the morning and afternoon, when a free cup of tea was provided. She made friends quickly, and a small band of four young ladies would go for a special lunch in the city, the Chop House restaurant in Farringdon Road, each payday. This had opened as a working man's eating house in 1869, and its meat-heavy menu was unashamedly filling and delicious. The girls looked forward to their outing with youthful, unbridled excitement, walking with speed from the lift—it was unladylike to run—locking arms and gabbing as they ran for the bus.

Rosie's main role was to type sales sheets and invoices. There were huge machines on the far side of the section that took paper as big as a small table. The sheets she typed would detail the consumables, e.g., 1000 cases of Trussells Cream. Her section looked after the Home

Counties, and she knew each field representative personally. Nestlé was a colossal business, especially for milk and cream products. Easter and Christmas were bountiful for Rosie's family as she came home with staff gifts of mouth-watering chocolate. Rosie was eager to learn about the company, and her genuine interest in its history was noted. Most staff just did their jobs and went home. But Rosie would visit the basement records in her breaks, rushing her cup of tea to immerse herself in the fascinating papers. Nestlé had a strong history, beginning in 1866 with a condensed milk called Fussells— to be known in later years as Carnation Milk— and the incorporation of the Anglo-Swiss Condensed Milk Company. As a tinned milk, it travelled well and had a good shelf life. In 1867, the founder, pharmacist Henri Nestlé, made a breakthrough in infant food: he combined cow's milk, wheat flour, and sugar and developed a formula for infants who could not be breastfed and whose mortality rate was high. This product was called *farine lactée* and, with its launch, the iconic Nestlé nest logo was created. Subsequent changes in company ownership saw Nestlé separate from Anglo-Swiss, but they merged again in 1905. With two head offices abroad, they opened an office in London to drive export sales with milk products (including sterilised milk) heading the product list.

During World War I, shortages of raw materials and difficult cross-border trading persuaded the company to add processing facilities in the USA and Australia to meet the increasing demand for condensed milk and related products, especially chocolate. From 1915, tinned condensed milk became an integral part of emergency rations for the military, and by the end of the war, Nestlé had forty factories and large government contracts.

In 1916, the company added a Norwegian business that had patented a spray-drying process for the production of milk powder, and this was added to the product portfolio.

After the war (1919), as the armies returned home the demand for tinned milk nosedived, and in 1921, the company faced a major crisis. They pulled back from that brink, but then, in 1929, the USA Wall Street Crash hit them hard as consumer buying stagnated. Nestlé took a gamble that chocolate would always sell and acquired the largest chocolate company in Switzerland, Peter-Cailler-Kohler, which was over one hundred years old and had a solid reputation. The gamble paid off and they thrived. They also continued to explore pioneering products.

In the aftermath of the Wall Street Crash, an interesting proposition arose for Nestlé, brokered by a mutual friend. The Brazilian government had coffee stacked in warehouses, but the price for coffee had collapsed. Could the coffee be transformed into soluble coffee cubes and sold directly to the public? Dr. Max Morgenthaler, a chemist, was recruited to help with the research. It took three years of research to find that, when converted into powder, coffee mixed with milk and sugar (café au lait) kept its flavour for longer. But the powder did not dissolve easily. Dr. Morgenthaler continued the research and, in 1935, he presented the first drinkable, soluble coffee samples to the executive board of Nestlé. This brought Rosie up to date, and she nurtured an affinity with the company that sparked her interest even further.

On 1st April, 1938, in Switzerland, the first supplies of this innovative product were marketed, and it was a great success: Nescafé instant coffee was born. Rosie would be an integral part of the launch in the UK. The representatives had little suitcases that contained a flask of hot water and the little sachets of the coffee. They canvassed companies, and orders came pouring in, like warm spring showers nourishing emerging crops. Rosie was so happy at Nestlé. She could use her intellect and her skills, and she blended in as if she were the hot water being added to the instant coffee. Her work and commitment led to her being offered a life-changing promotion to relocate to Switzerland. Her mind was engulfed with picture-book images of snow-covered wooden chalets, and she couldn't wait to tell Lily Eleanor. Her mother's simple but crushing reply was a firm, and final, "No." Rosie was devastated, and rushed out to the front parlour where she played with the piano keys to mask her sobs. She could not cry in front of her mother, and she knew that Lily Eleanor would not soften. Her mother's word was law.

Later, when she had composed herself again, Rosie called on Dorothy in Jamaica Street and was introduced to two soldiers who Dorothy's father had befriended in the street. With her father's admiration of uniforms, he was drawn to the two Scots Guards, found them engaging and invited them home for tea. For Rosie and Dorothy, two young men with charming manners and a soft Scottish lilt (and approved by Dorothy's father) were rather appealing, and when one of them asked the girls if they would like to go to the cinema sometime, they replied coyly, "If you like."

Rosie was certain that her mother would not agree to a date with a soldier, but when Lily Eleanor heard that Dorothy's father had recommended them, she allowed Rosie to go. Although this and future outings were casual, Rosie, who was deprived of male guidance due to the absence of her father and any male role model, (even her maternal grandfather, Robert, had died at the end of 1935), was energised each time a new date was confirmed.

20

The office at Nestlé was bustling. Sales representatives dropped by to check their orders, on edge as the huge machines processed and deposited the magic numbers that would guarantee them a good wage packet that month. Chunky Bakelite telephones rang intermittently, whilst the productive *click-clack* of the typewriters made music with the *bing* of the bell as the end of each line of type was reached.

Seventeen-year-old Rosie wondered what she had done wrong when her boss approached her desk and asked her to come to his office. He was young for a manager, only twenty-seven years of age, but he came from a good family and was polite and refined. He was tall and slender with light brown hair; not a 'looker', as Rosie and

Dorothy might have mused in their girly chats, but smart and pleasant. Inside his office, he closed the door, cleared his throat, and said, "Rosie, would you like to come to the theatre with me one evening?"

There was a ten-year age gap between them, but in those days, it was not unusual for older men to court younger women. Rosie was so relieved that she wasn't in trouble and allowed a modest smile to develop as she replied, "That would be nice, but I will have to ask my mother's permission."

He was smitten with Rosie—her bearing, intelligence, and her endearing naivety. Rosie had never been to the West End of London and was keen to accept. But she had to ask permission from Lily Eleanor who grilled her with questions. Finally, Lily Eleanor said, "I will let you go this time, but you will be back when I say." And that was her permission obtained. Rosie was used to the rigamarole of seeking permission and could feign listening if necessary to speed up the ending, whether the result was yes or no. She accepted she had little influence over the final decision.

Rosie's admirer lived in Kingston-upon-Thames, and they had a maid in their house. His father was 'something in the War Office', and his brother was a master in a big school in the north. Polar opposites, but Rosie was not distracted by class; her granny Elizabeth Emily had taught her decorum and manners.

During the ensuing months, Rosie enjoyed the young man's company and the indulgence of the West End as they visited a theatre or a cinema once a week. He knew that she lived in Stepney, but this was not an issue for him, except that he could only take her to the bus stop at the end of each evening as he had to catch a train back to Kingston. Rosie did not believe that he avoided going to Stepney, but her mother began to imagine unfounded malevolent intent. He asked Rosie to his home for tea and the live-in maid served their tea in the lounge where they found conversation easy and pleasing. Rosie was not in love yet, but there were stirrings of a budding relationship, and she genuinely liked her beau. She went out with other boys, normally in a foursome with Dorothy, but he was progressing at a faster pace and had taken to leaving small presents on her desk, one being a powder puff in an ornate case with a red rose gracing the top. He was clearly intent on winning her affections, but the presents alarmed her mother and strengthened her fear of the worst.

"Why is he buying you things?"

"Why doesn't he bring you home?"

"He must only be after one thing."

"You cannot see him anymore."

Rosie was upset and had to refuse his invitations. In the absence of a proper explanation, he was bewildered and a little angry but kept his distance. But Rosie was only seventeen and would soon bounce back. But the office environment would never be the same again, and she did miss what they'd had.

21

"We are moving into the pub in Moody Street."

This was the bombshell that exploded for Rosie during 1937, a year pitted with highs and lows. Robert and Sarah's pub in Shoreditch had been identified for slum clearance in 1934, and the brewery had offered them a choice of two pubs to take over. The first was in Poplar and the second in Mile End, which was much nearer to Gold Street and Edmund's family. They decided to take the pub in Mile End. Bessie and Edmund would serve in the bars whilst Robert and Sarah managed the business. Eva, the cleaner, came too, like a lapdog blindly following and clinging to its master. But it was a long trek from her Shoreditch tenement.

The pub was The Bancroft Arms in Moody Street, Mile End, on the corner of Bancroft Street. It had a sweeping bar and attached off-licence and a smaller bar where the women tended to go. It was a beer house selling beer and cider, both draught and in bottles. No spirits were sold. They did not serve food but did have pickled eggs and other nibbles on the bar counter.

Robert had died in 1935, aged 73, and Sarah had continued the management of the pub on her own. At the time, these changes had little impact on Rosie and Ted, other than their father being at home more often (he could no longer make excuses to stay away overnight). But Edmund had already relinquished the role of head of the house and remained more of a guest than a functioning father. But now it was 1937, Sarah was ageing, and she wanted Edmund and his family to move in and take over.

Rosie was distraught. She had spent her whole life in Gold Street. It was her world, her sanctuary, and her inspiration. Her paternal kinsfolk were a joyful extension to her nuclear family, and she was happy. She was further distressed by her pledge to the Band of Hope which her mother had ensured was imprinted in her brain, as if a quill pen had scratched in the mantra with indelible ink. Her pleas were summarily dismissed, and Gold Street soon became a memory. To Rosie, even Granny Elizabeth Emily and Edmund's extended family were abandoned and had abandoned her: they did not visit the pub. Sister Lily Blanche was married and living in Plaistow, so the move had little effect on her, and Ted did not seem to mind; he was doing well at work and enjoying his daytime apprenticeship. The family dynamic though, was irrevocably changed, as if an invisible mole was burrowing through its foundations and gradually weakening the entire structure.

The move was not just physical. Lily Eleanor's independent community life was cast aside, and she was thrust into servitude, working in the bars with Edmund and her sister Bessie. Her freedom of movement was repressed: she could no longer visit the almshouses or wander the markets but did still help in the church whenever she could. However, her money-lending activities (which had been small but regular) increased with the customers in the pub, and her relationship with her sister began to blossom.

Lily Eleanor served in the small bar where the ladies bought their stout and sat awhile, a brief escape from the hardship of daily life. 'Rabbit Pol' was a particular character. She earned the nickname as she always had fresh rabbits for sale. She would come into the bar with a fresh rabbit and exchange it for a bottle of stout, which she would sit and savour whilst engaging in banter with the other ladies.

Edmund and Bessie served in the larger bar, which was so big it went round a corner with Edmund also looking after the off-licence, where people came for bottles of beer to take away. The pub was open every day except on Christmas Day, when it only opened at lunchtime (Christmas dinner was always served in the evening.) The pub's opening hours controlled their lives. Even with the long opening hours, Edmund would still be called downstairs after closing time by people rapping on the off-licence door and trying to buy beer. Rosie felt that they had become enslaved to the community.

Rosie mourned the loss of her childhood home, and her grief was fuelled by the news that the Baker family had taken over the tenancy. She felt a deep sorrow in the fact that the old familiar rooms, the sanctuary of the kitchen and her special place on the window ledge in the parlour—where the walls had absorbed her music—would soon be saturated by the miasma of boiled greens, fried herrings and fetid nappies, and that the bright red doorstep and polished brass knocker would fade into despondency.

Whenever her mother allowed, Rosie would go out, and in the absence of the outings with her beau at Nestlé, she continued to go out with her best friend Dorothy and Rosie's casual soldier admirer, Bill. Soldiers were a no-no, a taboo to Lily Eleanor, but when Bill said he would visit the pub, Rosie had to tell her mother that he was a soldier, but quickly reminded her that she had been introduced to him by Dorothy's father, which placated her mother in advance of the first meeting. Bill had tattoos, which were another no-no for Lily Eleanor, and Rosie warned Bill not to take his jacket off when in her company. He had two large pen and ink tattoos, done in the Army, one on each forearm. The first depicted a Red Indian in full headdress, and the other, a Scots Guard, with the bearskin headdress. Bill was in the Scots Guards, and his regiment wore the bearskin headdress, which was eighteen inches tall and weighed 1.5 pounds, and which, in those days, was made from the fur of the Canadian black bear. He was part of the Queen's Guard, infantry soldiers assigned to sentry duty, and he was often on duty at Buckingham Palace. After a few beers, he might mention some shenanigans he witnessed which were resolved through the back door at Buckingham Palace. But he was fiercely loyal to the monarchy, and even with a loosened tongue, he would not go into details.

A COCKNEY ROSEBUD

It is a matter of public record that the issues at the palace related to the Prince of Wales, who was to become King Edward VIII and who later abdicated to marry Mrs. Wallis Simpson, an American divorcee. He had a reputation for womanising and reckless behaviour. Alan Lacelles, the prince's private secretary for eight years during the 1920s/30s, recorded that: *for some hereditary or physiological reason, his normal mental development stopped dead when he reached adolescence.*

Bill was a charmer, with warmth and charisma; tall and slim, with jet black hair, a ready smile, and a seductive Celtic lilt. Everyone who met him liked him.

He had had a tough childhood, which over time he shared with Rosie, and Lily Eleanor. He was born in 1915 in Perth (Scotland), and he signed up at eighteen for four years Colour Service with the Scots Guards to escape an abusive and unhappy home life. His father had emigrated to America, promising to send for his family, but his mother Catherine never heard from him again. There was a big age gap between Bill and his brothers and, when his mother tragically died of cancer, they were able to fend for themselves, whilst he was still a child. An aunt took him in, but she was cruel to him and gave him very little. At times, he didn't even have boots for his feet. He was very bright, and school gave him hope, although he was forced to leave too early, aged only twelve years. He had to earn some coppers wherever he could and he could not wait to get away. Joining the Scots Guards in 1933, he was soon stationed in London and, after suitable training, on sentry duty at Buckingham Palace. He was a private man, intelligent and gentle, and with a meaningful understanding of deprivation. He would give his last coppers to someone more in need than him.

Bill was transferred out of Colour Service to the Reserves in December 1937. He was based in Pirbright, Surrey, at the Army Training Centre and would visit Rosie and the pub whenever possible. Rosie stood little chance of deflecting his allure. After Lily Eleanor had spent time with Bill, she grew to adore him, and Bill felt that he had found a true family: people who cared about him. Rosie was always allowed to step out with him, but there was one problem: he never had any money. Salvation for their nights out came in the guise of Edmund, who, once installed in the pub in Mile End (and an important figure in the community), was often given free cinema tickets. There were three cinemas: the Troxy, the Palladium, and the Coliseum, and Bill hoped that Edmund would have some tickets when Bill was on a pass. The Palladium and Coliseum both closed in 1938, restricting the availability of the perks and resulting in more time being spent in the pub, but at least Rosie could sit and talk with Bill and try to accept the life that she now had.

Rosie did not enjoy living in the pub—the family quarters were soulless, and nothing was familiar. The piano was relegated to a corner, minus the goldfish, and covered with a sheet. And the warm, cosy cocoon that had been the family kitchen, with the eternal coal fire and gently boiling kettle, soon became a distant memory. The pub was also noisy: the constant hum of voices, the clinking of bottles and glasses, the cigarette smoke, all permeated the rooms as if the building absorbed the DNA of its customers, like a burgeoning monster. But Rosie was a teenager, enjoying work and a social life, and that made this new existence bearable. What other choice did she have? She had at least exhaled the lingering smell of boiling greens and putrid nappies from her nostrils.

The living accommodation in the pub was upstairs, with the typical outdoor toilet and washhouse in the backyard. Inside bathrooms were rising in popularity, and they were life-changing (and often a conversation topic in the bar). No more treks in the dark with a candle or (if you were lucky) a torch in hand to a perfunctory, cold, draughty, uninviting, outdoor toilet with an antiquated flushing system and a surfeit of spiders and other creepy crawlies. There was a room at the top of the stairs in the pub that seemed to scream to Rosie, "Bathroom, bathroom, make me a bathroom!"

But Lily Eleanor was unmoved and refused to entertain the idea. It wasn't a question of money. Simply she had always managed things the way they were, and that is how they would stay: weekly visits to the Community Baths with daily washdowns at the kitchen sink. The room remained a storeroom, and after a while, its voice quietened to a whisper and then disappeared altogether.

Rosie missed watching Granny Elizabeth Emily cook and listening to Aunt Elsie's piano playing and soft, soulful singing. Granny had encouraged Rosie to learn from her, something that held no interest to her mother, and Rosie had been commended on her pastry making—a great compliment from a master baker. A move of only a few miles had uprooted the railway track of her previous life and shunted her into a semi-abandoned railway siding.

22

The air has warmed; snow has lost its icy grip and the rhythmic beat of the quickening thaw plip-plopped to the ground whilst the droplets ricocheted around the tree trunks and bushes; sodden earth was trampled underfoot as the snowdrops said farewell, and the grey sky silently popped like bubble wrap being burst by tiny fingers, revealing those little hints of blue. Winter was retreating, the frozen earth was beginning to stir in preparation for the release of dormant life; and in tandem with nature, the excited sounds of children playing in the streets and up The Waste, returned to the East End.

Life in the Bancroft Arms had its routines. However, during 1938, they knew that war was coming, and this dominated talk in the pub bars. Memories of World War

I had only just faded, with many still bearing the scars and the aftermath of war, battles, and deprivation. Despite the threat of another war, it remained a priority to improve housing and health in the East End of London, and in 1939, Rosie's Aunt Lizzie, who had always lived with Granny Elizabeth Emily, was allocated a council house in Dagenham, Essex. Her husband, William, was a Dock Foreman at the Port of London Authority, and the threat of war where the docks would be targeted hung over the family like a wrecking ball, slowly gathering momentum. They relocated to Dagenham (some 15 miles from Stepney) with their son, Norman, Aunt Elsie and Granny Elizabeth Emily, leaving Gold Street behind to physical demolition. But bricks and mortar did not house the lifetime of memories—these were in Rosie's soul.

Estrangement was inevitable. The close ties forged from living just a few doors away frayed when Rosie was moved into the pub and stretched to breaking point when the nucleus moved from the locality. Family ties were weakened again by the death of Sarah, Lily Eleanor and Bessie's mother, in January 1939, aged 75 years. It was significant that the licence for the pub was transferred to the two sisters, Elizabeth Florence (Aunt Bessie) and Lily Eleanor, and not to Edmund. The women in the family were the business and finance managers. Sarah left a tidy sum, including stocks, and the women would look after it. They were financially secure, but their lives were threatened by the looming war. However, the 'Phoney War' came first.

In September 1939, there was a *blitzkrieg* (a German word for a lightning war) attack on Poland. The Germans hoped to disorganise its opposing forces by using mobile armies and locally concentrated firepower. Poland was now occupied, but in Western Europe, nothing of military importance was happening. War had been declared by the Prime Minister, Neville Chamberlain, during the morning of the 3rd of September, 1939, but so little happened from then into spring 1940 that evacuated children began returning to their parents, and the expression Phoney War was coined. Rosie knew some of the young men who signed up at only fourteen and fifteen years of age who boldly declared: "It will be over by Christmas."

A chilling similarity to the start of World War I.

Rosie was keen to follow her father and her Uncle Wilf's example in World War I and went to the WRNS (the Women's Royal Naval Service – officially known as the WRENS) recruiting office. Lily Eleanor was apoplectic. No discussion, just a thunderous, "No, you are not!" as she turned on her heels and dismissed Rosie's feelings, yet again.

Ted joined the Royal Air Force and spent the whole war in India. As a serving member of the Scots Guards, Bill was assigned to dig trenches in Hyde Park, and Lily Blanche stayed in Plaistow. Her husband Harry did not join the forces. He wasn't cleared medically, so they continued to visit the pub, and Lily Blanche would help behind the bar on occasion. Rosie was excited and proud to find out that her Aunt Elsie had joined the newly formed ENSA (Entertainments National Service Association) and had gone to France to entertain the troops. She dreamed that she might join her. Of course, it remained a dream.

Behind The Bancroft Arms was a railway line. It was also near the docks, and big guns had been mounted by the railway line in defence of air strikes. Locals referred to these guns as 'Big Berthas', but this was not strictly true. The Big Bertha was a German Siege Howitzer, deployed in World War I. A Howitzer is a big gun—rather like a small tank—that can turn in any direction and fire high into the air. The nickname Big Bertha came from the German newspapers and spread to Allied servicemen as slang for all heavy German artillery, especially the biggest 42 cm guns. The adults in the East End knew this slang only too well, and it was soon back in use for the big guns positioned at the railway line. Rosie saw the guns so close to the pub as a death sentence waiting to happen.

*A Big Bertha Gun,
courtesy of Fedor Sidorov and Shutterstock.com*

With war declared and everyone in fear of their lives, relationships changed, dreams were suspended, and aspirations deferred indefinitely. A single day, each day, was the only priority. Rosie and Bill married in June 1940, a quiet affair in The Christ Church in Jamaica Street where her sister had married a few years earlier but with significantly more optimism. This would be one of the last weddings to be held in the church: it would be one of the first casualties of the London Blitz and never be rebuilt.

Rosie and Bill's Wedding in 1940. From left to right, Lily Blanche, Ted, Bill, Rosie and Aunt Bessie

After getting married, Rosie had to leave her job at Nestlé. Another life track relegated into the railway sidings. They lived in the pub, but Bill was on active duty. Rosie was lonely and frustrated. She had lost her job for her husband, but he could not comfort her. She would get a postcard occasionally, and then a message that he had 24-hours leave, and he would come home for a day.

Rosie was never expected to serve in the pub. She would look after the living quarters and do the shopping and washing whilst waiting for Bill to come home. She did a lot of knitting, keeping her brain active and the unthinkable at bay. She had long since abandoned her music. She had lost her mentor and her private space to practise. Energies were concentrated on survival, and that would be their daily life for many years to come.

23

Sirens wailed, blackout curtains were hastily drawn, and people scurried to safety whilst searchlights danced in the darkened sky. It was the 7th of September, 1940, and the London Blitz had begun. The Phoney War was history. Life would never be the same again.

At first, the German bombers concentrated on military and industrial targets, but after the Royal Air Force retaliated and hit Berlin, the bombing of civilian areas in the UK commenced. The Germans were preparing to invade and occupy Britain in a military operation they called Operation Sea Lion. It was vital in this campaign for them to gain air superiority.

On that first night, over 350 German bombers crossed the English Channel from France and dropped

300 tonnes of bombs on the docks and streets of the East End of London. Rosie thought she had been transported to hell, with each ensuing night recreating a terrifying limbo.

The government had provided some 'Anderson' shelters, and 150,000 were given to households who had gardens to put them in. They were poorly made of corrugated iron and were cold and damp. The best that could be said about them was that they were better than nothing; but the pub did not qualify to receive one anyway.

Many people felt safer in their homes and took shelter in the understairs cupboards. This was Lily Eleanor's favourite. Mothers put their small children in cupboards. There was also a 'Morrison' shelter that was simply an iron cage that doubled as a table and, during an air strike, a family could huddle under the structure as the building collapsed around them. The force of an air strike was unknown at the time, and the use of a Morrison shelter had not factored in heavy rubble landing directly on and around it, hindering escape not only from the building but any resulting fires. They became death traps of their own.

In the West End of London, underground clubs provided shelter, but mainly to the well-heeled, affluent residents. But even wealth could not work its magic on the rooms as they quickly became unwholesome and urine-soaked. Stepney Green Underground Station was already a working train station, with additional stations being built along the train line, and was used as an air raid shelter. This was not initially supported by the government as they wanted transport to be left clear to help move troops, and some station entrances were closed with barbed wire before nightfall, but they were powerless to stop the thousands of petrified East Enders seeking safety. They would buy platform tickets when necessary to gain entry, and then camp on the platforms, and during the night, on the train tracks themselves. Bona fide travellers using the trains just picked their way around them and tried to avoid stepping on the bedding. Stories that reached the media tended to depict a positive picture: crowds of smiling faces listening to an impromptu concert, hot drinks being provided on exit in the mornings, and groups of shelterers chatting and playing cards. The dark, dank spaces around them were just a background to the parties. This was perhaps true in the bigger London stations, but not in Stepney. The reality for the East Enders was overcrowding in damp, airless tunnels, without adequate ventilation but with the ever-present risk of infectious diseases including flu, tuberculosis, and pneumonia being spread. Children developed a condition coined 'shelter throat' from the unhealthy atmosphere in the shelter, followed by being turned out in the early morning to the damp mist and the smog lingering from yet another night of bombing and burning buildings. Their clothes were always damp, and their houses cold from a shortage of fuel and money. Lily Eleanor and Rosie hated going to the underground shelter. It was packed, noisy, and stunk from the filth that was unavoidable. Yet it was in use every night throughout the Blitz and beyond. It provided a measure of comfort for the terrified population that their houses and streets could not.

Even underground stations could take direct hits, with fatalities. In early 1941, 50 people were killed when a bomb blast ripped through the ticket hall at Bank Station. No refuge could be regarded as safe.

Between the 7th of October, 1940, and the 6th of June, 1941, 92 high explosive bombs and one parachute mine fell on the district of St. Dunstan's and Stepney Green. A parachute mine is a naval mine dropped from an aircraft by parachute. The attacks always came at night, but fear was an overwhelming emotion twenty-four hours a day.

The devastation is hard to comprehend. It was impossible to walk anywhere without seeing abject piles of rubble, buildings partially or totally demolished, and huge craters. And there were so many fires. Familiar streets with name plaques crumpled and scorched morphed into wastelands of rubble and detritus, and Rosie dared not dwell on the fatalities. She once saw a trolley bus upended in a crater in the road. It was impossible to put out all the fires, and they had to be left to burn. The air was filled with choking dust and ash. Children no longer sang and played hopscotch in the streets or laughed as they ran to The Waste. Childhood was cancelled.

Devastation in London.
Courtesy of Everett Collection/Shutterstock.com

24

As history shows, the British defences held, and Adolf Hitler quietly cancelled Operation Sea Lion but not the bombing raids. The East Enders strove to ensure life as normal during the day against poor odds, but they didn't give in. If a shop premises was damaged, the shopkeeper would move outside into the street. The community was determined to find hope, however deeply buried in the deadly chaos.

Rationing had started in January 1940, but only for bacon, butter, and sugar, which were core dietary items of the time. Pubs left standing were essential for a short respite and boosting community spirit. If deliveries were interrupted, Edmund would go—sometimes miles away—to buy bottles of beer to serve his customers. People deserved relief from the terrifying, nightly onslaught. The intensive blitz of London officially ended in May 1941, but the bombings continued throughout the war, including daytime attacks.

As the days and months slowly edged into years, not only the landscape changed—the sky was veiled with the constant rise of grey dust from bombed buildings, and the blackened smoke of eternal fires. If a tree or patch of grass survived, it was impossible to recognise the season with no birdsong or the joy of a balmy breeze. Everything was grey, drab, and spartan, like a silent, under-funded, grainy black and white film from the cinema.

Rosie dreaded the raid warnings—a tocsin of impending death. Having the Big Berthas behind the pub and being near the docks, the sirens could be first, or second to the hooter from the Ford Car plant in Dagenham, if the planes were approaching from that direction. Sirens made a loud and long signal of warning. If for alert, the siren had a pitch that rose and fell. For an all-clear, it was a long continuous sound. An alert did not always mean a raid followed. And, conversely, raids could happen without an alert being sounded. People were worn ragged—one of Hitler's objectives—and would take chances 'cocking a snoot' at the Germans by trying to live some form of normal life. But it was still the early days of war.

25

There is magic at twilight, that time when the sun falls gently below the horizon and sunlight is scattered above, sharing its shimmering glow below. Is it day or is it night?

Rosie had loved to sit on the windowsill in Gold Street and watch the pretty sunset as she quietly hummed a ditty or two. Looking out of the window in the pub, twilight was a host for the curls of smoke rising from burned-out buildings and the precursor to dread at impending nightfall. In the pub there was always a dog. Regardless of sex, each dog was called Bess. One Bess loved a bowl of tea with a sugar cube positioned in the middle, and Rosie didn't tire of watching the ritual attached to the treat. Bess had to see that sugar cube and lap her way towards it with eyes fixed on the prize, not just pounce on the sugar. It was uncanny that, if an air strike was imminent, Bess would howl before the sirens went off. When the sirens sounded, Edmund would insist that Rosie make her way to the shelter, calling up the stairs, "Off to the shelter, Rosie, NOW!" Customers hurriedly made their exit, leaving half-empty bottles of beer, but draining their glasses. Lily Eleanor and Bessie would go to the cupboard under the stairs. Edmund would make sure his till and his stock was safe before heading for the pub cellar.

Hastening to the underground shelter one night, Rosie felt compelled to glance upwards and, in the darkened sky, she beheld a fleet of German planes in tight formation, intent on achieving their deadly mission and unafraid of the powerful beams of the searchlights that swept and swivelled through the sky as each wave of aircraft thundered through. The beams picked out individual bombers and, transfixed, Rosie could see flares dropping, which is how the pilots lit fires to guide their soon-to-be dropped bombs. The too familiar sound of the Big Berthas could be heard, but what chance did they stand? It was a grotesque arcade game: shoot one down, and three take its place, without interruption. Following The Thames River to reach the docks, Rosie's small community and the pub became a regular target. Rosie's fear was palpable. The odds of the pub escaping a raid were decreasing, and the proximity of the docks facilitated the growing likelihood that a German bomb would deliver its death sentence very close to home.

With the concentrated night-time Blitz over, life became a little more tolerable. When Bill was home, he and Rosie would sit upstairs in the pub during the evening, listening to the radio and playing cards. Radio was their lifeline, not only for news and developments, but for entertainment and some much needed laughter, provided mainly from American recordings. Comedy programmes such as the Chase and Sanborn hour with a stand-up comedian and The Pepsodent Show with Bob Hope and a host of rotating stars and musicians of the time, such as Judy Garland and Desi Arnaz with his orchestra, had their audiences laughing in abandonment. There were newspapers, of course, but Lily Eleanor had been instructed by her parents never to read the 'News of the World', a Sunday newspaper. It was far too scandalous and racy, concentrating on crime, scandal, and vice and was not allowed in the home.

Bill never talked about war experiences, and Rosie would only find out years later that he was sent to Northwest Europe for two months in April 1940, and that his ship was sunk—with fatalities—on his return from Norway. He needed to forget.

If Bess gave Rosie and Bill a heads up, they would switch off the radio, pull the blackout curtains shut, and turn off the light as they headed for the shelter, arm in arm, but at a pace. These routines had become the new normal.

26

The new normal continued through 1941 and into 1942. Everyone lived with war—the unwanted and abhorrent trespasser. No one made plans, and dreams remained in translucent suspension. Many prayers were said, and perhaps some were answered. The plaintive cry of a newborn did not, however, come to the pub in Moody Street in August 1942.

Standing at the trolley bus stop in Mile End Road, feeling poorly, with swollen legs and feet that could only fit into slippers, Rosie was making her way to the London Hospital in Whitechapel. Other travellers were disinterested, hardly giving Rosie a glance: living with war and the constant fear of its terrifying consequences, they had hardened hearts. She was heavily pregnant, but things were not right. Lily Eleanor's solution was to send her daughter to the hospital on her own. Bill was on active duty. Lily Eleanor had ceased to worry about Rosie being snatched from the streets, never to be seen again, and was busy with the pub. Her lack of overt motherly love wasn't a surprise to those around her, but Bessie and Edmund did raise their concern, which Lily Eleanor dismissed with, "She's going to the hospital. It's not far. They will look after her."

With sheer determination, Rosie walked from the bus stop to the hospital entrance, which had many steps to navigate, and on entering the reception area, she was at last treated with compassion and eased into a wheelchair by an orderly. The hospital was built with a warren of tunnels underneath that housed the boilers and equipment that kept it functional and, due to the risk of a bomb strike, these tunnels were being used to transfer patients and provide some measure of safety. As Rosie was gently pushed along, she felt an overwhelming tiredness sweep over her and in a semi-conscious haze, she imagined that she was navigating the long journey to heaven. It was a surreal experience.

Rosie did not go home that night, nor the next, or the next. But no one visited. Pregnancy and childbirth were not considered an illness and Lily Eleanor held the view that no news was good news. Rosie had preeclampsia, a serious pregnancy-related high blood pressure disorder. There was a danger that her high blood pressure would reduce the blood supply to the baby. Untreated, both the mother and baby could be harmed. She was in the right place, and in that respect, Lily Eleanor was right. There weren't any phones, but there was still a degree of community spirit and the Bobby (policeman) from the pub's local beat was asked by Lily Eleanor to enquire at the hospital and relay the news back to Rosie's family.

Rosie gave birth to a daughter on the 18th of August, 1942: a beautiful blond-haired, blue-eyed doll. She was a little small but healthy and perfect in every respect. Lily Eleanor and Bessie eventually came to visit. It was a short visit where Lily Eleanor looked at the baby and gave her verdict saying, "She is very small." That was a truth, and Rosie knew her mother well. In the warm glow of new motherhood, Rosie shrugged off the comment. Her daughter was here and real. Lily Eleanor could not take that away from her. With Bill being on active duty, he did not see his firstborn beauty until she was seven months old. Rosie registered the birth and chose to honour both Rosie and Bill's mothers by naming her Eleanor Catherine; this was shortened to Ellen in everyday company. Eleanor sounded a little formal for the tiny bundle.

Lily Eleanor did ensure that Ellen had a bed until they could get a second-hand crib. Raw materials for manufacturing were routinely ear-marked to support the war effort so spreading the word that a crib was needed was the only way to find one. In the upstairs living room, she emptied a large drawer, put it on top of the sideboard and then lined it with bedding. It was only Edmund, however, who gave the cuddles.

27

Blond curls hanging loosely around her ears, a mischievous smile whilst skipping along in her bright-red siren suit—called a playsuit or a jumpsuit today—Ellen was the apple of Edmund's eye. She loved to play behind the bar, and her favourite game was to mix up all the bottles on the shelves: it would keep her occupied for hours. The bottles were arranged in a specific order, so Edmund could just reach behind the bar, without turning around, knowing exactly where the right bottle would be. But no more! Was Ellen chastised? Of course not!

Ellen loved her siren suit, which was a mini version of the leisure suit designed by Winston Churchill in the 1930s, although the sobriquet siren suit was not given until World War II. Churchill was often photographed in a siren suit which was loosely cut so that it could be put over other clothes at speed, rather like workmen's boiler suits but more stylish. They came into their own during the war, as they were really easy to throw on when an air raid siren sounded and people rushed to the shelters. And so, the nickname was coined. For tomboy toddlers (and their mothers), the siren suit was indispensable.

Ellen was a living doll. One day, Rosie had to take her on an underground train journey. Wearing a pink dress and bonnet, with her blond curls just visible and her vivid blue eyes, which sparkled when she smiled, she walked confidently up and down the station platform, waving her little hands and beaming at everyone, while they waited for the train. The other travellers were in awe of such prettiness during such a dark time. It was a brief reminder that beauty did exist despite the ugliness that war presented. Ellen's innocence was adorable, and it comforted their souls. They all wanted to take her home.

During World War II, women also started to wear trousers for the first time, but not Rosie; Bill did not like women wearing trousers, and Rosie had always worn dresses and skirts, just like her mother. Rosie would take Ellen out in a pram for the family rations. Prams were functional with a sturdy build on large wheels, a mattress and weather hood for the child and with space underneath to place groceries. Ellen's pram was of course second-hand. Until they ended up as shabby props for children's games up The Waste, prams would pass from family to family, as needed. They were part of the community too.

Rationing covered most foods by 1942 and was a way of life with long, snaking queues outside the shops. But there was a pleasant camaraderie among those waiting in line. You had to take your own newspaper or wrappings and reuse everything you could. Rationing was strict but necessary, and people coped, eking out a bit more by having a few chickens or growing a few vegetables—none of which was possible in the pub. This was the level of weekly rationing for one adult in 1942:

Bacon & Ham	4 oz
Other meat	equivalent of 2 chops, or 1s 2p
Butter	2 oz
Cheese	2 oz
Margarine	4 oz
Cooking fat	4 oz
Milk	3 pints
Sugar	8 oz
Preserves	1 lb every 2 months
Tea	2 oz
Eggs	1 fresh egg and an allowance of dried egg
Sweets	12 oz every 4 weeks

Anyone with a baby in a pram always got a little bit extra tucked in with the baby like a magic trick, perhaps an extra egg or two, and Rosie was often chivvied to the front of the queue; but no one minded after receiving Ellen's smile.

Air strikes still happened with regularity, but after three years of war, Rosie was tired of the rote pub existence and the underlying dread of Bill not returning. Her mind was stagnating and stimulation was in short supply, so she would take Ellen out for walks in the pram as often as she could. The landscape was lugubrious, a dull grey of devastation and ruin: no more pretty parks and gardens through which to wander, no seasonal flowers to admire or bird song to lift her spirit. But being in the open air was preferable to the oppression of the pub, and she could enjoy a chat with anyone she met.

And then it happened. No sirens. No warning. No stampede of people or Bess, the dog's warning howl. Rosie was strolling along, pushing Ellen in the pram, when she heard a familiar but deadly noise. It was a sole German Bomber, but it flew so low and so close that she could see the front gunner sitting in his glass bubble beneath the pilot, guns pointing downwards. There wasn't any time to run, or any point with the superior speed of the plane, but Rosie was not paralyzed with fear. After three years of unrelenting bombardment, she knew in that split second that, if today was the day, then so be it. She was weary of the absolute control that war paraded. She stopped walking and looked directly at the gunner as the plane flew towards her and he commenced firing. Such is the hatred of war. He was not going to spare a young mother and her child. But his wish was not fulfilled. His shots missed, and Rosie survived. But many others did not.

28

Wednesday the 3rd of March, 1943, was a typical evening in the East End. Beleaguered residents lived on despite their fear. Families sat at home with their loved ones, listening to the radio and daring to talk about life at the end of the war. Cinemas provided respite, captivating their audiences in a world of singing, dancing, and entertainment, if only for a few hours. Noisy, smoke-filled pubs supplied their customers with a convivial refuge and an opportunity to curse the enemy. But that night, the close-knit community would be brought to its knees—and not as a direct result of Adolf Hitler and his bombers' actions.

The Bancroft Arms was humming when several wardens burst in, their faces streaked with dirt. Choking back the tears burning a path down their dirty cheeks, one of them blurted, "There has been a terrible accident in Bethnal Green Underground Station."

The underground station at Bethnal Green was not operational as a train station but had been used as an air raid shelter for some time. For most locals and visitors, it was the preferred shelter, and thousands had used it hundreds of times, particularly women, children, babies, and the elderly. When the sirens prompted evacuation after dark, the entrance became a problem. It was narrow at only 15 feet x 11 feet and, because of black out regulations, there was only one 25-watt light bulb to guide the way down nineteen steps to the first wider landing. Add a big crowd of people, and the light became ineffective, obscured by the mass descent. It was like descending into the bowels of the earth. But despite its rank smell from overuse, it was a place of relative safety and people had used it time and time again.

On that fateful evening, a combination of factors conspired to rival Hitler in its tragic outcome. The first factor had been the need for greater speed to get to the shelter. In 1943, the East End was facing lighter, faster German bombers and people had less time to get to safety. The second and key factor, however, was the launch of new defensive anti-aircraft rockets: British rockets designed to protect the locality. Their sound resembled the heart-stopping whirring and buzzing sound of bombs dropping. After three years of bombardment, it was a sound that everyone recognised.

When the sirens sounded that evening, there were already five hundred people in the shelter, with one-thousand-five-hundred starting their descent into the underground station. Most were on foot, but three buses also offloaded their passengers at the entrance to the station. Only ten minutes after the sirens sounded, sixty of the new anti-aircraft rockets were launched in quick succession. The fear that bombs were already falling spread through the crowds like static electricity discharging its electrons, arcing from body to body, compelling the recipients to move even faster. It wasn't panic, but the increased speed caused an even bigger bottleneck at the narrow, dim entrance. The third factor added its own, hidden, detriment. It had rained that day, and the steps down from the pavement were slippery. Anxiety was bubbling in the crowd and soon people were stacked like sardines in a huge tin, trying to get to the shelter entrance. The swell was relentless, and determined to move forward, but as a woman carrying a child reached the first landing—after safely navigating the nineteen steps—she lost her footing and toppled over. The man behind was so close that he was unable to stop himself from toppling over her and, in just fifteen seconds, the domino effect involving over two hundred people resulted in a stack of helpless bodies in an area no bigger than a small room, wedged and unable to move. Their screams were silenced by the sheer weight of the people on top of them, squeezing the air from their lungs. It was a night of abject horror. Rescuers had to crawl over bodies in their frantic attempts to get to those poor souls at the bottom. And no air raid happened. Not one bomb fell that evening, yet 173 people lost their lives: 84 women, 62 children and 27 men. It was the worst single incident of civilian loss recorded throughout the entire war. For the community, the impact was profound and devastating. Underground stations had been their refuge; a place of relative safety. Trust was shaken, the dead mourned, survivors and rescuers comforted, but life had to go on. Lily Eleanor would never go to an underground shelter again, but she still insisted that Rosie went with Ellen; it had to be better than nothing.

29

In June 1943, Rosie took lodgings in Longmar Road around the corner from the pub. It was two upstairs rooms rented from the landlord—one with a sofa, a small table, and 2 chairs, and the other room with a bed and a chest of drawers. There was a gas cooker on the landing, an outdoor toilet and standby tap for water. She borrowed a couple of pans, crockery, cutlery, bed linens, and towels from her mother, and took her knitting and some books. She yearned for privacy, to be freed from the chains of her mother's dominance and to develop a closer relationship with Bill when he was home. She still spent time at the pub when Bill was on active duty but had independence for the first time in her life. It was a new and satisfying experience to make her own decisions. It didn't matter that the war thwacked innovation and creativity; she felt in control of her life for the first time. In early 1944, her sister Lily Blanche, by then the mother of two young boys, was evacuated to Wales—to the Rhondda Valley— to work in a munitions factory. The government paid her wages and her accommodation under a formal contract. She was housed with a family who looked after the boys while she worked. Her husband Harry helped in The Bancroft Arms during her absence.

Life in the pub carried on. They had become so used to living with war that the fear of death was repressed as they went through their daily routines, like hamsters on their rotating wheels, waiting for someone to open the cage door. Lily Eleanor developed rheumatism in her knees, and Edmund still suffered with his chest, but they were chugging through. Ted was relatively safe in India, and Lily Eleanor was banking the £7 a week Ted got from the RAF to provide for his future when he returned. But then Bill needed help.

30

The rocket flew straight and level towards its unsuspecting target. Servicemen and civilians were participating together in morning worship, and the choir had burst into song, the euphonious voices masking the tell-tale buzz of the V-1 rocket, launched from France. The momentary silence, a characteristic of this type of rocket, was lost to the congregation, attentive in their worship as the rocket cut out and nosedived into the roof of The Guards' Chapel in Birdcage Walk, SW1, near to Buckingham Palace. It was a direct hit. The roof, supporting walls and concrete pillars concertinaed, swiftly creating tons of rubble, whose immense weight sealed any potential escape route. It was catastrophic. The only way in was behind the altar, and medics on site scrambled in to help.

It was Sunday, the 18th of June, 1944, 11:20 am. The instrument of death was one of the first V-1 rockets to be fired at London. It took 48 hours for everyone to be freed, and the death toll was high: 121 soldiers and civilians and 141 seriously injured. The Guards' Chapel belonged to the Wellington Barracks, the headquarters of the Scots Guards, where Bill was stationed at the time. He was in his bay when the rocket hit, and his stomach lurched as the deafening noise pervaded the bay. Was the bay next? Was this his time? He heard, "Take cover, take cover," and then the voice of his senior officer, with a simple, but explicit, "Leave NOW and don't come back for 48 hours."

The men rushed outside, and even through the billowing clouds of dust that choked the air, they could see the horror and hear the dreadful screams of pain and suffering. Bill knew that some of his friends had been in the chapel, but orders were never questioned, and they left.

Rosie was upstairs in the pub listening to the radio when Edmund called up the stairs, "Bill's here. You need to come down. Now." Rosie thought his tone was odd and rushed down to find her husband slumped in a chair, head down and shoulders cowed, but jerking uncontrollably. He wiped his eyes with the back of a trembling hand. She took his damp hand in hers. She had never seen him cry, and overt displays of emotion were uncommon in her family, so she just sat and looked at their clasped hands. The pause seemed interminable. Edmund busied himself at the bar. When Bill had calmed down a little, he related what he knew about the bombing and described the scene of carnage.

"I couldn't help my friends. If there is a God, how could he allow this to happen?"

The bombing had infiltrated Bill's growing emotional vault. Like a slithering viper winding its way inside this quiet, thoughtful man, preparing to rise, coil and strike, the split second the vault opened. The sinking of his ship in 1940 when he was returning from active service in Norway, the fear as he clung on to flotsam in the cold water—he wasn't a good swimmer—and the soldiers lost. They were men that he knew. The death of a friend on active duty, knowing that a bomb could wipe out your family in a heartbeat, and the general horror of war were edging him to a rupture. Rosie had been denied the understanding of the depth of Bill's emotional turmoil; he kept such feelings to himself. Returning to the barracks after 48 hours, he witnessed the lines of covered lifeless bodies and felt an internal pain that one hundred aspirins could not have touched. The viper had struck. He functioned like a hollow shell, carrying out the routines of years of training and then, on the 7th of July, 1944, he went AWOL (absent without leave). He went missing for eight days. He did not go home to Rosie but returned when his mind was calmer and his loyal, reliable character shone through again. He had little memory of where had been. He was arrested and put on a charge, which, when the full circumstances were heard and with his previous long and unblemished record, resulted in a supportive path of ten days of detention and a forfeit of six days' pay. Bill returned to active duty, and Rosie remained oblivious to the whole episode.

To support psychological recovery, The Guards' Chapel was reopened in time for the Christmas services of 1944 with the full rebuild scheduled for 1962 to 1963. It was sorrowful that over two thousand small commemorative plaques in dedication of Guardsmen lost since 1660 were destroyed. Casualties for a second time.

31

Rosie was expecting her second child in late September 1944 but felt better during this pregnancy. Ellen was nearly two years old and growing fast. They spent time in the pub but hurried to their lodgings when Bill was home. The rooms were sparsely furnished, and they just had clothes and necessities, but being together as a family created its own ambiance. Her accordion, the piano, and the bulk of her personal belongings were still at the pub, including jewellery, which would be safer there. It was difficult to secure belongings in a shared house. Rosie did bring one special item. It was a silver-plated replica *Titanic* cruet set that her mother had found in a market some years before. The ship base held a salt shaker at one end and a pepper at the other, with a mustard pot and teeny mustard spoon in the middle. Mustard was powdered in those days, and you mixed it with water in the mustard pot when required. Rosie had been both saddened and fascinated by the tragedy of the *Titanic* sinking and would daydream about life on board in the luxurious surroundings, whilst stirring the mustard ready for their meal. With meals in The Bancroft Arms now perfunctory and hurried around the pub's opening hours, the ship cruet barely left the cupboard, but Rosie remembered it. As it graced the little dining table in their lodgings, getting a daily buff and shine like the brass knocker she used to clean in Gold Street, Rosie could imagine she was dining in a swanky restaurant. Air raids were frequent, and her uppermost fear, especially when on her own with Ellen, was to hear the buzz of a V-1 rocket followed by the unnatural silence. You knew its lethal journey was ending. But not where it would fall.

V-I rockets were shaped like a small plane but unmanned, fuelled, and fired at Britain, mainly from launch sites along the French and Dutch coastline. They were known as Buzz Bombs, or Doodlebugs. Because they flew low, straight and level, they could be destroyed before enacting their murderous purpose using land-based defences such as anti-aircraft guns and by defensive fighter planes in the sky; in advance of running out of fuel and nosediving into a target. The Barrage Balloon also proved to be a worthy defence against these rockets. Resembling huge, innocent string puppets, these balloons were a deterrent against any threat that was low-flying, like aircraft and rockets. The cables, like puppet strings, held the bobbing mass in the air and posed a great risk to both enemy planes, which were piloted, and V-I rockets which were not. Flying low to avoid detection by home fighter pilots, both aircraft and rockets would career into the Barrage Balloons' cables, get tangled up, and explode in the sky. Today, these balloons can still be seen, high in the sky, but as an advertising medium such as the launch of a new shopping arcade.

From the 13th of June, 1944, when the first one was successfully launched by the enemy, to the last one on the 27th of March, 1945, 2340 V-I rockets hit London, resulting in 5475 fatalities and 16000 injuries. However, many lives were saved by 3500 V-Is being destroyed before reaching a target. The Royal Air Force concentrated on tracking the source and bombing the launch sites, the final one in range of Britain being taken out of action in October 1944.

The V-2 rocket first launched against Britain in September 1944 and was even more deadly, with about 1400 falling on London alone. The V-2 rocket was the world's first guided ballistic missile and was unstoppable. No defence could destroy them, and it took teams from the Allied Forces—USA, United Kingdom, France and The Soviet Union—to seize the German manufacturing units and the technology and destroy the launch sites to halt the carnage. Their accuracy was inferior to the V-I, but they travelled at the speed of sound and lacked any distinctive warning noise. Many people were deceived in the early days, believing that the explosions caused by the V-2s were gas explosions, and not a result of bombing attacks. Official reports that reached the East End of London provided some comfort and understanding that the tide of war was turning and that Germany was at last on the defensive. Any uplift for Rosie and her family, however, was soon to be swept into oblivion.

After the attack on The Guards' Chapel in his Wellington Barracks, Bill feared for Rosie and Ellen's safety.

His priority was to get Rosie, who was seven months pregnant by then, and Ellen, to a safe place and outside of London. He talked to Rosie about going to Scotland and staying with his Aunt Jessie. Rosie knew about the childhood cruelty to Bill, but together they rationalised that Rosie was an adult and could handle herself if the need arose. It was the only solution available, so Bill contacted Jessie by telegram. She agreed in a brief reply and tickets were bought for Rosie and Ellen to take the train to Scotland. On the 18th of July, 1944, her identity card was stamped with her new address. Identity cards had been introduced by the National Registration Act of 1939, and everyone had to carry one and keep it up to date. Jessie, however, meted out an alternative type of cruelty by changing her mind just before they boarded the train. She did not want the bother, especially babies. So, Rosie did not go. They were distraught, but without a plan B, they had to stay in London. The Germans, however, had other plans.

32

The silence was inescapable, her mind dulled and her teary blue eyes were unable to blink. Gripping Ellen's small chubby hand almost too tightly and holding a small suitcase in the other, Rosie stood on what had been the corner of Moody Street, bewildered and lost. The Bancroft Arms was gone. Shaking her head a little to bring back some feeling, her lips quivered as she looked around, feeling like a lost child, waiting for someone to say, "It's ok, we've found your parents." Determined not to let go of Ellen's hand, lest she disappeared as well, Rosie let her eyes sweep around the desolation, trying to penetrate the smoke and ash that filled the air around her. Surely the pub was just hidden in the smog, right?

"It's just a nightmare," she told herself. She would wake up; the pub would rise from the ashes, and she would run inside.

"Please God. Please God. PLEASE God!"

It was the night of Saturday, the 29th of July, 1944. The Battle of Normandy was underway, and the Americans were pushing back the German offensive. There was hope for victory at last, but that dreadful night, Rosie's world imploded. It had been a typical night in the pub: Edmund and Bessie were serving in the large bar and Lily Eleanor in the small ladies' bar. Harry (Lily Eleanor and Edmund's son-in-law) was visiting and helping out behind the bar and in the cellar. The talk was animated and positive, and the customers timidly optimistic. They knew that the Germans were retreating and, for the first time in many years, there was a chance that life would return to normal. Lily Blanche was in Wales with her boys. Ted was in India. Bill was on active service, and Rosie—heavily pregnant and finding the smoky pub atmosphere oppressive—was in the lodgings knitting and listening to the radio, whilst Ellen slept beside her on the sofa, nestled in cushions and a blanket.

In The Bancroft Arms, Bess began howling. The sirens sounded, and the lights went out on the railway line behind the pub. A raid was coming. Hearing the alert, Rosie scooped up Ellen and made her way to the shelter at Stepney Green Underground Station, dreading the smell and the filth but recognising the foolhardiness of staying in the lodgings. She was now responsible for more than just herself. In the pub, the patrons began to leave. The V-I Doodlebugs had only been used in raids for just over a month, and many had been shot down, so although people were preparing for the raid, this type of attack did not cause undue worry. Air raids had been central to their lives for four years now, and their reaction was routine: Lily Eleanor and Bessie made their way to the understairs cupboard, whilst Edmund and Harry headed, as usual, to the cellar.

They may have heard the buzz. They may have discerned the ominous silence as the V-I rocket ran out of fuel, cut out and nosedived towards its target—usually the docks nearby and the railway line behind to disable the Big Bertha guns. No one will ever know. The pub took a direct hit and, in seconds, The Bancroft Arms on Moody Street, E1 was a grotesque pile of rubble, engulfed in a thick cloud of dust, as if trying to hide the reality of its demise. The death sentence had been enacted.

If only Lily Eleanor and Edmund had gone to Clacton on Sea and opened their off-licence. If only Robert and Sarah had chosen the pub in Poplar. If only, if only, if only.

Rosie was unaware of the tragedy until the all clear sounded and she came out of the shelter. Walking back towards her lodgings with a sleepy Ellen in tow, both coughing as they inhaled the thick mist of smoke and ash, she saw a level of destruction in her locality that she had never seen before and fires burning all around. Her heart started pounding, the beats resounding in her ears as she hurried towards Moody Street, to the familiarity of the pub and her family. She told herself that, of course, her mother would have gone to a shelter and not to the cupboard under the stairs. But deep down she knew that wasn't true. The cupboard had provided safety for four years, and she was unlikely to go anywhere else.

She walked on in a daze, treading familiar pavements but disconcerted by the lack of familiar buildings and street corners as she neared Moody Street, and The Bancroft Arms. She stopped at what had been a familiar street corner, and the buildings were gone. She stared in disbelief and disassociation. Brought back to reality by the sounds of the rescue teams, Rosie picked Ellen up and held her tight whilst she cried out to the people trying frantically to move the heavy rubble and reach those lying underneath. But they could only shake their heads and look away.

Lily Eleanor and Bessie were found, their bodies intact and undamaged by the missile, but killed by the force of the blast that expelled the air from their lungs. Harry was killed in the cellar by the collapse of the building, and his little boys were only ten months and two years old respectively, but Edmund was dug out alive. Everything was gone. Rosie's past was erased in seconds, all her personal belongings gone. The talented young woman, full of dreams and aspirations, died that night. She would never stretch her fingers across a piano keyboard again or lose herself in the music of her accordion. All photographs were lost to her and her children, forever. No reminiscing through photo albums and keeping history alive. The enemy's far-reaching hand had torn the heart and soul from her body. The cockney rosebud would never reach full magnificent bloom.

A few items were salvaged, including some pieces of jewellery, but Rosie never saw them. Her father and brother lay claim to anything that was found. She was able to see her mother in the temporary mortuary, which was full of trolleys shrouded with white sheets tracing the outlines of what had been living, vibrant people only hours before. She was still in numbed disbelief. The pillar of her existence had gone. The figurehead of the family was lying prone on a trolley. She seemed asleep, her face relaxed, but she was stiff and cold to the touch. Amongst the other mourners, whose pitiful wails filled every molecule of space, Rosie found her thoughts difficult to grasp. They were not racing, but strangely absent. She felt limp and empty, as if her essence had been sucked out of her. But she had to be stoic for Ellen, and the soon to be born baby. All Rosie could do was mourn her mother and move on. Standing by her mother's side, she whispered, "Goodbye, Mum," and made to leave but turned back when she thought she heard her mother's voice, "Rosie, is the money safe?" Hesitating slightly and glancing around to see if anyone else was talking, a thought dropped into the abyss of her mind: *The money belt. What about the money belt?* Lily Eleanor never removed it and hid it under her clothes. It would have gone with her to the mortuary. But Rosie didn't dare remove the shroud and search her mother's clothes in front of the other mourners. She would mention this to Edmund, unaware and unable to countenance that it was her father's first thought after being rescued from the ruins. She would never hear about the money belt again.

Bill was informed by the authorities, but he was still under arrest and could not be given leave. Rosie believed he was still on active service somewhere. He was heartbroken—it was like losing his own mother again. He cursed the war but was thankful that his wife and child had not been in the pub that evening. At least they had the lodgings and a few belongings, but he was becoming desperate to get them away from the daily death and destruction that haunted their community, and unable to make the escape happen. Edmund was untroubled by their situation and, thinking only of himself and Eva, he took refuge in Harry and Lily Blanche's house in Plaistow, which had not sustained any damage. His only communication dealt with the funerals: he made the arrangements and settled probate. Lily Eleanor had left a comprehensive will and a substantial financial settlement, of which he was well aware, but Rosie was not. Aunt Bessie (Lily Eleanor's sister), left her own will that was handled by her executors. Rosie never knew what it contained.

Edmund was not prepared to wait for the money and added to Rosie's emotional turmoil by knocking on her door and pleading that he could not afford Lily Eleanor's funeral costs, asking for money. Rosie was seven months pregnant with only a few articles of clothing to her name, but she believed her father's magician face and parted with a few precious pounds. She did not think about the large sum of money idling in an account for Ted, of which her father was well aware.

Lily Eleanor's estate was detailed and healthy. She had included funeral expenses—essential because of the war—and £48 was paid out for her own funeral, and £32 for Harry's. Edmund got a tidy sum in savings, stocks, and the bank account, and the three children should have got £194 each. Rosie did not know and never saw a penny. Her father's true character was revealed. Rosie and Bill's circumstances would have been eased with her rightful inheritance, but Edmund was consumed by his own selfishness and his burning desire to fulfil his life with Eva. Nothing could hold him back now.

33

It was vital for Rosie to leave London. She went to the authorities, pregnant and with Ellen beside her, clutching the hem of Rosie's coat as if her young life depended on it.

"Where do you want to go?"

Rosie bristled. "I have nowhere to go, that is why I am here. I have nothing in the world but this suitcase. Everything else has gone. I thought you were here to help?"

Rosie was just another grey statistic.

"We will issue you with an open train ticket, and you can go wherever you like," was the response. "That's all we can do."

She put the ticket in her pocket and, back outside in the street, determined to find her sister in Wales.

On the 8th of September, 1944, Rosie arrived in the Rhondda Valley. The host family for Lily Blanche allowed her to stay with her sister, but in the absence of a formal evacuee contract it was necessary to find somewhere else for Rosie to live. The baby was due at any time, so Rosie stayed with her sister for three months. Lily Blanche had not been able to attend the funerals of her husband, Harry, or her mother, so having Rosie around allowed both of them to grieve, to talk about the family, to reminisce and to forge a type of sisterly bond they had never experienced. After the new baby boy named Alan was born, Rosie moved in with the family of a Mr. James: a father, son, and an uncle. This arrangement was accepted in the community as Rosie was an evacuee, had two young children, was married and the locals knew her as Lily Blanche's sister and a reputable young woman. She kept house for the James's in return for lodgings. The two men worked down the mine. They were very kind to her, and she was content.

Rosie was happy in Wales. She felt safer there than she had the last five years. Her sister worked at the munitions factory, so Rosie saw a lot of her two nephews, and they played with Ellen and their new cousin, Alan, who was born on the 27th of September, 1944. Dark-haired like his father, Alan was an easy baby who, as he began to crawl—with navy blue knickers over his nappy—was always covered in coal dust, and always cheerful. All the local men worked down the mine and got a daily ration of Player's Weights cigarettes, as if coal dust wasn't bad enough for their lungs. As Ellen and Alan were too young for school, Rosie often took them out in a pram. It was a real community that brought back vivid memories of Gold Street, and Rosie found the residents very kind and welcoming. It made being separated from Bill easier. The docks were nearby and, in the evening, some of the houses would open wide their living room windows and sell fried fish and chips, the fish being straight from the docks. Rosie would lick her lips as the gorgeous smells wafted around the streets.

34

Although World War II ended in May 1945 with the unconditional surrender of Germany, the official signing to end this harrowing war took place on the 2nd of September, 1945. Rosie had been in Wales for nearly a year and had lived in an impenetrable shade of grey for six years with fear a constant bubbling just below the surface. The release was uplifting; like having a yoke removed from her shoulders and being able to stand tall again.

They returned to London with their children, and Rosie stayed with Lily Blanche in Plaistow whilst the search for a place to call home was undertaken. Bill was due to be demobbed from the Scots Guards and was actively applying for a home, as were thousands of soldiers returning to the ruins of their communities. The authorities were installing prefabricated homes (prefabs) to ease the housing crisis, and Bill and Rosie applied, only to get an instant rejection letter dismissing their application as the prefabs were for London County Council tenants only. Rosie was born and bred in Stepney but was rejected at every turn and was in despair. As he was a regular soldier and not a conscript, Bill went to his commanding officer for help. He intervened and secured accommodation for Rosie and Bill in Dora Street, E14 (Limehouse). Left with no other choice, they moved in on the 15th of September, 1945. The accommodation was a 'Nissen Hut', designed and used for temporary military barrack units. It was just a huge sheet of metal, bent into a half cylinder and buried into the ground for stability. It had a couple of windows punched out and some basic essentials: a stove, a sink, a tin bath and rudimentary electricity. The long, lugubrious space was deemed fit for residential occupation. There was, of course, the inevitable outdoor toilet and a water standpipe. To affect a homely appearance, each hut was given a front gate from the road, and a little garden at the back.

Rosie and Bill came to the hut uncluttered, without possessions or spare money. But salvation came from a personal visit from an officer of the Scots Guards who had known Bill for many years. No other authority would help, and they could have been sleeping rough in the streets, but Bill's regiment was looking out for him. The officer visited many times and single-handedly got them basic essentials like beds, a kitchen table, and some chairs. But more importantly, he made them feel worthy. On one occasion, he brought two American generals with him in a Jeep. Rosie was dazzled and adored their accents and affability. They gave Ellen and Alan an American dollar each. Rosie never found out what the children did with the dollars; she never saw the dollars again, but she never forgot the officer.

35

The Nissen Hut was dire. They lived in this dour metal shed for three years, but with renewed spirit and determination, they created a home inside, tilled the garden to grow some vegetables and acquired some chickens for fresh eggs.

Bill was demobbed, and they lived together as a family for the first time since their marriage. And for Bill, it was the first real family setting he had experienced. As if Rosie had not seen enough coal dust during her time in Wales, Bill secured a job at the Gas Works in Bromley-by-Bow. This is where the processing of coal took place, producing not only coke for industrial and domestic use, but gas for homes. Coke is a small, grey, hard and porous coal-based fuel produced by heating coal at high temperatures without air. It has few impurities and replaced coal in domestic homes and industrial units where smoke-free fuel was required— that is, clean air zones. It was heavy work and involved 24-hour rotation shifts, but at least he had work and an income.

Household tasks were challenging with washing done by hand and water constantly on the boil for hygiene and cooking. With two young children happily frolicking in the dirt outside and Bill's job ensuring that his work clothes were grimy, the tin bath was also in constant use for bathing and washing clothes. It was impossible to keep food fresh, so shopping and cooking was done daily. The hut, being made out of metal, was difficult to heat during the winter, and conversely difficult to cool down during the summer, when the inside temperature bordered on sweltering. But even the lack of basic privacy in this dismal space could not dent their joy in finally being a family unit.

Ellen was three when they moved in and Alan just one year old. Alan was a mischievous imp. He was a jolly baby who loved to dig holes in the garden and bury things. Rosie was always losing cutlery and she never found the commemorative *Titanic* cruet set that mysteriously went AWOL. It was probably cosying up to the American dollars. Her experiences during the war years had taught her to value relationships over possessions, so although a little sad at losing the cruet set, she did not dwell on it.

It was a blessing that the children could be outside. It wasn't much of a garden, but it was much safer than the bomb craters and detritus they had left. Rosie even managed to grow a few flowers. The days and months passed. They had a radio and played cards, and Rosie knitted furiously. They were happy to be a family but dreamed of better accommodation. As a cook, Rosie had inherited the natural talent of Granny Elizabeth Emily. She had watched Granny cook so often and could play back recipes in her head, like a live cooking show with Granny providing the narrative. Nothing was weighed—she did not have any scales anyway—and nothing was wasted. When the wholesome soups and stews of her childhood were on the menu, she would switch channels to the recipes of her father but gave live eels a wide berth. She did compromise a little for Bill, though, and he would get jellied eels from the sea food stall as a treat; he loved them so much. Rationing was still in force and a way of life. Fruit and vegetables were not rationed, but they were always in short supply, so whatever they could grow outside in the garden was invaluable.

Rosie crafted a gorgeous shortcrust pastry—it just melted in the mouth, and Bill and the children would gobble it up greedily. She just threw a few ingredients into the bowl, although she always sieved the flour, mixed them with her hands, dropped the mix on the table, rolled it out, added it to the pie dish—covering steak and kidney, apple and clove or rhubarb—and would then balance the pie dish in one hand whilst she trimmed the pastry edge with a sharp knife. After squeezing her thumb along the pastry's edge as a seal, there would be a lavish brushing of milk to finish. The discarded pastry edging was not wasted and was twisted into shapes to adorn the top of the pie. A small slit was made by the pastry knife to ensure the pie funnel, shaped like a chicken and placed in the bottom of the dish, could let steam out during cooking.

Bill had to clip the wings of the chickens to prevent them from flying up into the trees or over into the next-door garden and, after the flush of laying was over, or if one was broody and not producing eggs, a chicken would be killed and cooked for dinner. Neither Rosie nor Bill could kill anything, so the milkman would do the deed!

The neighbours were superficially friendly, but if Rosie did not collect the eggs each morning before going shopping, they would be stolen. One day, someone pried open a window, climbed in and stole Bill's watch, which he did not wear for work. They had their suspicions but could not prove anything. It left a sour taste. These were difficult times, and people had so little. To take from your own neighbours, who also had so little, was unforgivable.

36

In September 1946, another son was born, the only one of Rosie's post-war babies to be born in hospital, as the Nissen Hut was unsuitable for a home birth. Thankfully, Rosie's preeclampsia was not repeated. She remarked that for her, giving birth was like shelling peas but that she suffered from after-pains (akin to extended labour pains) for the following five to six weeks.

Family rarely visited. Edmund visited occasionally to see his grandchildren, Ted called round once or twice after he was demobbed from the RAF, and her sister had remarried. Rosie never met her sister's new husband and only knew from her father that he was Irish. It was difficult for a young mother like Lily Blanche with two toddlers and no breadwinner, to keep afloat financially. Her mother was dead, her husband was dead, and her father was enjoying his freedom with Eva, so it was not surprising that she sought security and companionship with another man. Lily Blanche was aware of the dangers of her inherited heart condition and had been strongly advised by her doctor not to have any more children.

Whether it was the joy of release from the shackles of war, or the new husband wanting to have children of his own and not just someone else's, Lily Blanche became pregnant for the third time but died in childbirth in December 1946, aged only thirty-two years. The baby boy survived but was whisked away to Ireland very soon afterwards. The husband's family came over, emptied the house in Plaistow and returned to Ireland. Lily Blanche's two boys were bewildered. They were too young to take it all in. Their father had died, their new father had abandoned them, and their beloved mother was dead. Rosie wanted to take them in but could not have them in the Nissen Hut—there were already three children and two adults in the metal shed. Edmund said that he would take care of everything. And so he did. Quickly and skilfully. There was a short period where a relative took them in, but both little, lost boys were sent to an orphanage and then separated into foster homes. They never saw each other or any of their close family again. Edmund, their grandfather, who had been with their father when he died but had survived; Edmund, who pocketed all the family money and who had forged ahead from tricking children out of their pocket money, was unrepentant. He did not show remorse whilst irrevocably sending away his own grandchildren like clearing out unwanted furniture. How Lily Blanche would have sobbed and Lily Eleanor would have turned in her grave. If you cannot trust your father, who can you trust? "It's for the best," Edmund said, and that was his last word on the subject. Clearly the best for him. Rosie would never forgive him but was powerless to intervene. Her view counted for very little. And then he married Eva in October 1947, and she would inherit everything: the endless toil of Lily Eleanor, her sister Bessie, and their parents, Robert and Sarah would fund Edmund's new life, and he would make sure it excluded Rosie.

Rosie was not invited to her brother's wedding, although her father had briefly mentioned it on a visit. But in August 1948, there was a knock on the door. The small-framed female stranger standing there said, "I've come to tell you that your brother Ted and I got married."

"Oh, when?"

"Last month, July."

"And where?"

"In Hendon. That is where my family comes from."

And that was it. No social niceties, no goodbyes, and the lady left. It was ironic that her name was Grace. Rosie assumed she was driven by some sense of duty or that Ted had sent her, too weak in character to tell her in person. Sometime later, Rosie was sent a photo of Ted's wedding in the post in which Eva, now her stepmother, was in the line-up with Edmund and the bride's parents. Ted's only surviving sister, who cared for him throughout his childhood, was removed from the family album, discarded like old clothes. It was all about the money. Edmund and Ted colluded to keep everything for themselves, even the few possessions retrieved from the bombing of The Bancroft Arms, which were passed down through Ted's lineage. Ted kept very close to his father. He knew which side the bread was buttered. And they say that blood is thicker than water. Using the RAF wages saved for him by Lily Eleanor during the war, Ted and his new wife bought his sister Lily Blanche's house in Plaistow and lived there comfortably, buying a car and, over the years, improving the house. Rosie was deeply hurt by her brother's actions—she had no idea it was about the money and did not know about her mother's will—but her mother's indoctrination was stronger: never show emotion and carry on. Rosie displayed the bulldog spirit, whilst her closest relatives turned into wolves and hyenas.

37

The letter looked official. The envelope was embossed, and the name and address were typed. The postman had knocked and put the envelope in Rosie's hand, and she held it as if it was ancient parchment that could disintegrate if handled roughly. Her heart began to beat a little faster. The sounds of the children playing on the floor behind her muffled. Dare she open it, or should she wait for Bill to come home? It was addressed to Bill, so surely he needed to open it? Would he be annoyed if she opened it? What should she do? The fingers around the envelope were beginning to tighten so, without taking her eyes away, she swapped it to the other hand and smoothed out the creases. Clearing her thoughts with a shake of her head, Rosie put the envelope on a shelf, out of the reach of little prying hands, and continued with her day. She was unable to stop herself from glancing at the envelope every now and then, worried that it would vanish if she ignored it and praying that it contained good news.

The moment Bill walked through the door, the children bombarded him with, "Do your ears, do your ears, please Daddy, do your ears." Bill could raise his ears up and down without moving his eyebrows, and the children loved it. Rosie bustled whilst they had their fun and then retrieved the envelope and handed it to him. He glanced at the front and ripped it open.

"It's a house! It's a house! We have been given a house, Rosie!"

They had been allocated a three-bedroomed prefab on a new estate in the Essex countryside. Rosie had to sit down, and Bill whooped. He scooped up his young son, Alan, and whirled him around the room, with Ellen, by then a grown-up six-year-old, laughing from the sidelines and saying, "My turn Daddy, my turn Daddy. Please, Daddy." As his precious firstborn and his little living doll, how could he refuse?

It was an immediate occupation, and they had to accept or lose it. No problem there. Nothing would stop them from securing their dream. The next day, Bill went to the council offices, signed the papers, and the family packed for the move. This did not take long. They had many happy memories to take with them, but none in praise of the dank, dismal metal shed. They had so little time to prepare, and Bill was upset that he had to give away his chickens as there was no way of transporting them. They were not sorry, however, to leave a particular neighbour behind.

The new estate was called Debden and was a suburb of Loughton in Essex, on the edge of Epping Forest. They had been allocated a double prefab, which meant it had an upstairs floor with three bedrooms. There was an ongoing housing crisis because so many homes had been destroyed during the war, especially in London, and the influx of demobbed servicemen had exacerbated the desperate need for housing. Fast, innovative ways of supplying accommodation were a priority.

Prefabricated (prefab) denotes that it was manufactured elsewhere and brought to the site for assembly, like a monster build-your-own kit. Functional and without frills, the type that Rosie and Bill were allocated had a precast concrete slab ground floor with metal cladding placed over the supporting frame to the first floor. The residents nicknamed them the *tin houses*.

Rosie was ecstatic. Leaving the Nissen Hut was like emerging from a tunnel and seeing sunlight for the first time—a metamorphosis from captivity to freedom. When they moved in on the 20th of September, 1948, she was expecting their fourth child in the following January. And now they had an indoor bathroom with a bath and running water and a large, functional kitchen. The toilet was still outside—although by the back door rather than at the end of the garden—and it had electric lighting. There was an open coal fire in the living room with a back boiler that provided hot water—no more kettles and saucepans eternally simmering in the background —and, for the first time since they had welcomed Ellen into the world, a bedroom of their own. They also had a garden back and front. Nirvana. Despite the house design ensuring that it was freezing cold during the winter and boiling hot during the summer (it was the use of metal again), they understood their good fortune.

The house was also home to big spiders, huge ones with thick hairy legs. Bill was scared of spiders but could not harm them. If one was in the bath—and they seemed to use it as a watering hole—he would drape a towel over the side to ensure that it could get out. If there was a big one in the lounge, he would get a mug and a saucer, put the mug over the spider, upend it with speed whilst putting the saucer over the top, and deposit the spider safely in the garden, where it likely made its way back in soon enough. Rosie called each resident spider Fred.

A third baby boy was born on the 20th of January, 1949, weighing in at over ten pounds—Rosie's babies had got progressively bigger. And all the children were healthy and active. What could be better than a healthy family of three boys and one girl? Perhaps another dainty little girl?

38

The estate was well served with public transport, and Bill could get to work easily. But it was a long journey. He would walk to the railway station—which was on the Central Line Underground—and catch the steam train into Stratford, and then an underground train to Bromley-by-Bow, where the Gas Works did its magic and kept so many homes warm and functional. He worked a strenuous 24-hour shift rotation. The shifts were 6 am to 2 pm, 2 pm to 10 pm, and 10 pm to 6 am. He could make the 6 am start by getting the first steam train out. He got a day off between day shifts and two days off between night shift and the next day shift. He rarely had a Christmas dinner with his family unless his shift was 6 am to 2 pm. The job was dirty and physically demanding. He had overalls and work clothes that he would bring home for Rosie to wash, and they were black with coal dust. He would never travel in his work clothes and got changed at work. It was his Army training: he never left the house without shaving, cleaning his shoes, and slicking his dark hair with Brylcreem, even if popping to the off-licence for a few bottles of beer.

Being a Scot, Bill liked his whisky, and he liked to socialise, however fleeting. He had his local and would pop in to chat to the landlord, partaking in a quick whisky and water and gleaning all the local gossip. On the right shift, he liked to go into the pub nearest the Gas Works and have a wee dram or two before getting the train home. Rosie lost count of the times he fell asleep on the train on his way home and found himself still in the train carriage but in the railway sidings. The stop was the end of the rail line and the carriages would be shunted into the sidings until they were next used. Rosie never expressed anger about it—in fact, they used to chuckle about it—as he was a good father and provider and deserved his little respite.

She did fret when he was on the 6 am to 2 pm shift, though: if he went for his wee dram before coming home, he was lured into the Sainsbury's supermarket he passed by after leaving the station, and would come home with several carrier bags of goodies—items that were not necessary, but that the family loved—and could spend the whole week's housekeeping to boot!

Education of a sort was available for the children. The area was not prepared for such an influx of primary-aged children, but the council converted some barracks into a schoolhouse whilst a new school was built and ferried the children to and fro. The children were thriving, all healthy and happy—they finally had the solid foundations for a meaningful family life.

Such a suave couple!

39

Rosie was a homemaker and a good mum to her babies whilst they were dependent. Like a mama dog, once her puppies didn't need to suckle and could walk and explore, she found time for herself and developed some adult friendships in her new locality, if only for the odd cup of tea and chat. She had a particular friend, a Mrs. Daley, who, when visiting Rosie, dressed elegantly, had fresh makeup and a few sprays of a nice perfume. Rosie found her to be refined and with good manners. She had two sons who, tragically, had an inherited disorder, muscular dystrophy. It was tiring and emotionally draining for Mrs. Daley to care for them as their muscles weakened and also knowing that they were unlikely to live past their teenage years. The two ladies were united in their grief of what could have been. Their chats contented Rosie as her friend liked to read and was interested in current affairs. There was also the local gossip to ensure a bit of excitement. Rosie felt empowered to pat her face lightly with cosmetic powder and wear lipstick, and she began to introduce herself as Rose to new neighbours and shopkeepers. The new surroundings were enabling, and she started to bloom again.

She remained Rosie to Bill, who was able to charm his way through the complex labyrinth of her emotions to reach her soft underbelly. Neither was cognisant of how her mother's influence was bubbling beneath the surface with an occasional burst of her maternal ancestors' characters, like the random spurting of a hot water geyser, and the likely psychological injuries. Rosie had been raised in an emotional void, without real expressions of love, and this was her role model and deep-rooted understanding. Coping with the years of war, the loss of close family and the constant financial pressures from raising a large family had suppressed innate character traits. But for how long? Could the blossoming Rose overcome her genetic psychology? She had little interest in encouraging psychological development in her children. There was always too much to do, and they went to school, didn't they?

Their house was near Epping Forest, and it was Bill who would take the older children to play in the woods, introducing them to a world so different to the grey, uniform streets of Limehouse and the Nissen Hut. They were transported from barren patches of melancholy ground lost to the ravages of war, to the verdant resplendence of a forest with its noble trees, playful ponds, and inviting lakes. Many happy hours were spent playing hide and seek and catching stickleback fish in the ponds. They would buy rudimentary nets on sticks from the local corner shop for a penny and carry a jam jar with a string tied around the lip. There were whoops of joy when a stickleback was gently eased into the jam jar, then filled with pond water. But the children always emptied the jars back into the pond—it was the skill of the capture that was the game. There were newts in the ponds, but the children found them a little bit scary: too much like a baby alligator and too quick in movement. Back at home, they would chatter excitedly about their exploits. If Rose heard, she was too busy to acknowledge it. But she cared about their physical growth and nourishment.

There was a meandering street of shops, the Broadway, which served the growing estate admirably. In addition to an array of independent shops, including Pie and Mash, it had a big Sainsbury's supermarket with a luscious fresh meat counter. Rose had learned all the cuts of meat from Granny Elizabeth Emily and knew how to get the best meat at the cheapest cost. She loved beef but would never buy steak or the expensive joints, nor could she afford them. She would ask for a cut of beef called the *aitch bone*, which was incredibly cheap and provided two dinners for the family. When roasted, it was equivalent to having ribs, topside and steak in one joint. The aroma in the moisture-laden kitchen was heavenly as the oven door was opened to check progress and tiny globules of beef extract escaped with the steam. The resulting juices crowned Rose's expert Yorkshire Puddings and her rich gravy, thickened with Bisto, of course. As the juices cooled, a thick brown jelly would form, hanging invitingly to the underside of the white dripping and, the following day, the family would relish a bread and dripping supper: hunks of fresh bread from the bakery, lavishly spread with the mix of jelly and dripping. It was superb and nutritious. Paradise.

Rose could bone a breast of lamb, stuff and roll it, tied with string, and produce a Sunday roast for less than two shillings. Sainsbury's sold a large breast of lamb for sixpence, and Bill would be tasked with popping in to buy a couple on his way home before they were snapped up. Rosie would keep her fingers crossed that he hadn't had his wee dram that day. Food was the axis of the family dynamic.

The Italian ice cream parlour was a firm favourite with the children and Bill. When the pennies allowed, it would be a Sunday visit to the ice cream parlour for an ice cream sundae in a tall glass with fruit and cream on top. To get right to the bottom, they would give you a straw to suck up every last bit. Rose never accompanied them, but there was always a huge Sunday dinner waiting for them when they returned.

40

The pavements echoed as the excited children threw their stones into the crudely chalked hopscotch squares and hopped into play. Skipping ropes turned apace, the whacks sounding like a whipping as they hit the ground. Exuberant youngsters chased each other, playing tag, whilst others sat cross-legged on the rough surface, honing their skills with jumping jacks. This was a game where 6-pronged metal pieces, usually 10 in total, were tossed on the ground before the first player bounced a small ball amongst them. Before the ball had bounced twice, the player had to grab a jack, hold it tight, and catch the ball again. The game continued until the first player let the ball drop or dropped a jack. They were out and the next player took over.

The children loved to play outdoors, and at the end of the 1940s, it was safe. The biggest threat was scuffed knees. The youngsters in the council housing estate where Rose and Bill lived did not dwell on wealth and belongings. No one had a bicycle, although the occasional slightly battered push-scooter would trundle up and down with its owner, hotly pursued by a bunch of children shouting, "Let me have a go!" There were few motor cars, and the roads and pavements outside the tin houses were ideal components for the simple games that ensured plenty of exercise, laughter and friendship, and the occasional spat. Rose would watch the games through the living room window, whilst she tackled yet another basket of ironing. It brought back memories of playing up The Waste.

In June 1951, Rose and Bill completed their family with the home birth of a longed-for second girl—not so little though, weighing in at 11 lbs. Whether or not Edmund had mellowed and regretted his behaviour towards Rose, he did want to visit his grandchildren and had come to the tin house on occasion, but never with his wife Eva. Rose was always pleased to see him. She was unaware of the extent of his malevolence and would not find out for many decades to come. He came to see the new baby girl in the summer of 1951, but died on the 28th of September, 1951, aged 62 years, of acute bronchitis and heart failure. Rose and Bill briefly attended the funeral in London, but Rose had little desire to linger with Eva and her brother, Ted.

Rose and Bill were blessed with healthy, robust children, but it was challenging to provide for a family of seven. Rose was adept at managing the household budget, and nutritious food was always put on the table.

But she had to be creative to manage other aspects, such as clothing. She would look at the local noticeboards and visit jumble sales for all their clothes, not just for the children, and would queue before they opened to get the best picks. There were always books and toys to be found as well. Rose despaired at the rate the boys grew. It wasn't too bad when they were in short trousers, but once they were into long trousers, it seemed that each new school term, they needed new ones. But she was a competent seamstress, so she could repair minor rips and tears and, of course, she could knit jumpers and gloves. Many 'tally' men (debt collectors) knocked at the front door offering tick (slang for credit), especially for clothes and household items. Rose paid a small amount weekly into a clothing scheme run by a distributer in Stratford. She was able to pay in what she could afford each week, and when the pot was big enough, she would take the underground train to Stratford to browse the vast warehouse of clothes. The Provident Cheque was another credit facility that provided instant cheques that were valid in certain shops. These were for bigger or multiple purchases, and agents called weekly for the payments. Rose considered the interest element too high, but they were a useful backup in an hour of need. Fuel was always an issue. The fire was needed to heat water and the living room, and dry clothes in poor weather. If they ran low before Bill's pay day, he would carry home a bag of coke from the Gas Works to tide them over.

There was also the growing problem of space. With three boys and two girls and only three bedrooms, the boys were sharing and subject to the normal squabbles of brotherly love as they developed their distinct personalities. Rose and Bill put their name down for a transfer to a bigger house. The council had an exchange scheme, so if someone wanted to downsize, it was easy to swap. In 1954, the family of seven moved into a four-bedroomed house in an older part of the town.

It was a semi-detached brick house with a red doorstep that Rose had to ensure was cleaned and painted regularly, a legacy from Gold Street, and a tin of the vivid red paint sat on the cold tiled floor of the larder, ready and waiting. There was a wooden front gate with seven concrete steps leading down to the pathway in front of the entrance door and a steep driveway to the side, with its own gate. This would not be used until the two eldest boys passed their driving tests.

The house was big but had its faults. The window frames were metal, single-glazed, and draughty. The only heating was the coal fire in the lounge, which, in addition to heating the hot water through the back boiler, backed onto the kitchen wall and kept the kitchen warm. The windows iced up indoors during the winter nights and left puddles of water on the windowsills as they thawed. If it was a bad winter, the ice on the windows did not even melt during the day. The hall and stairs were difficult to heat, and Bill had to place a paraffin heater at the foot of the stairs, which the children had to avoid knocking over and whose smell lingered in the atmosphere. It would be some years before they could afford a stair carpet. The bathroom was an ice box, but too small for an independent heater, so Bill installed a light that had a circular heating bar around the base, but its use was restricted because of the fear of rising electricity bills. Woe betides anyone leaving it on. In a huge step forward for the family, it had a toilet in the bathroom, as well as a second toilet outside the back door in an enclosed back porch.

There was an airing cupboard outside the bathroom that housed the immersion tank, seasonally heated by the coal fire and by electric in the summer. It was toasty in there and warmed the towels as well as airing the clothes. There were four bedrooms: two double rooms and two single rooms. Rose and Bill had a double, as did the two younger boys with single beds whilst the eldest boy was given his own single room. He was 10 years old. The two girls shared the other single room, sharing the same iron framed double bed from the tin house. It dominated the small room.

Downstairs, there was a large kitchen with ample cupboard space and a larder with a marble slab for meat and dairy. This led through a doorway to a dining room with French doors opening to the garden and an archway into the front living room, which had huge, metal, draughty windows. This archway was destined to divide the family. Saturday afternoon football was an exclusive club. The men of the house commandeered the living room without a thought for anyone else. Bill had his old army blanket, well-worn but serviceable, and this would be draped across the opening, held at either end with strong tape fixing the hem to the wooden surround. Then the curtains would be drawn in the front living room. The men would enter their cocoon and watch the televised football matches, whooping and shouting from 1 pm to 6 pm. If anyone—the females, that is—lifted up a mere corner of the blanket, they were shushed and shooed away, unless bearing cups of tea. The women were relegated to the kitchen to tackle the massive weekly wash. Then Rose would cook dinner. On cup final Saturday, the 'boys' club' would exercise its squatting rights even earlier. However, the shops were very quiet on that day, and Rose would take a number 167 bus to Ilford and visit

Bodgers, a department store, and C&A's clothing emporium. Bodgers was similar to Wickhams in the Mile End Road, but not as grand. The trips flooded Rose with memories. And then there was the television programme, *Your Life in Their Hands*. This was a groundbreaking medical documentary series, aired in 1958 with ten half-hour episodes but running for five series until 1964. It covered serious surgical procedures from the view of the patient as well as the surgeon. It became another reason for the living room to be out of bounds. Rose and Bill were enthralled. They closed the curtains, turned off the main light and pushed the stiff switch of the standard lamp, waiting patiently in the corner for such special occasions, made a cup of tea and hunkered down to watch the wonders of developing medical practice.

The back door from the kitchen opened into a small back porch, with a coal store to the left and an outdoor toilet to the right. The back garden was a good size, with lawned areas to both sides of the concrete path. Bill installed a washing line that stretched almost the whole length of the garden and visited the local wood yard for a clothes-prop. In essence, just a long piece of wood, but with the important 'grabber' cut into the top to push against the line and raise the washing line up high. There was always a full line of billowing washing out unless it rained. In that case, the washing was dried on a wide wooden clothes-horse that surrounded the hearth. But you needed to turn the clothes regularly as the fire could be fierce and it was easy to scorch something.

Bill was keen to grow vegetables, but Rose's forte was flowers. She nurtured beautiful roses, geraniums, chrysanthemums, and carnations, all without a greenhouse. She worked on her palette of colours like an artist visualising their next canvas. Passers-by would stop by the front gate to admire and comment. She could take a small cutting from any plant, from her garden or out in the woods, stick it in some compost, water it and it would grow. She only bought plants if she needed a new colour. The front garden was Rose's artist's studio, and when in bloom, would rival any rainbow that a zephyr might coax down from the sky. Rose loved to have fresh cut fragrant flowers in the house. The rose bouquet was tender on the senses, a soothing balm caressing the nasal passages. You could smell the fresh blooms the moment you entered the house.

It was not perfection, but the house and garden were Rose and Bill's palace. Even with little money, they would nurture and knead their identities into its core, like softening leather with Neatsfoot oil, and be proud to call it home for the next three decades. They felt their good fortune.

The kitchen soon became the hub of the home with Rose cooking and baking. The children and Bill enjoyed every mouthful. They acquired an expandable kitchen table—a simple laminate top on wooden legs—that sat four people when closed, but had dropdown leaves at either end that opened and shut with a metal clasp. This enabled the whole family to sit down together, although Bill was often absent due to work and his feast would be placed in the warm oven for later. The one sitting was for practical purposes. Once a meal was ready, it was served immediately. Everyone ate, then Rose would wash up, make a cup of tea, and take a deserved rest in the living room with her feet up. On return from school, and until the meal was ready, the ravenous children would raid the food cupboard and take slices of bread to allay their hunger whilst they played outside.

41

Food and home were inseparable and dominated their lives. The weekly shopping was like an Army manoeuvre, subject to advance planning and meticulous execution. The bulk was carried out on a Friday afternoon after the older boys were home from school and could help. There was a significant challenge in the shape of a big hill. Traps Hill was a lengthy, steep link road from the older part of the town to the High Street. It was easy to go down, but demanding to ascend with its long, steep curves, especially with full bags of shopping. The bus stop was at the bottom, just into the High Street, but buses didn't go up the hill. Rose did eventually get a cavernous shopping trolley on wheels with a long metal handle. It had a robust golden brown wicker basket, so big you could fit in a child and a jaunty, patterned plastic rain cover. Full of shopping, you had to be strong to pull it. As it aged and the wicker deteriorated, it caught your clothes and snagged Rose's stockings, but it held an amazing amount of produce, and for the children, it was like dipping into an enormous bran tub of treats when it arrived home.

The first stop was the grocers. It was called Williams Brothers and had two discrete areas inside. To the left was fresh produce: meats, cheeses, butter and cream, and to the right, sundries such as tea, coffee, rice and flour. To the rear there was a booth that was raised up a few steps and it had a large glass-covered opening where a cashier sat and settled the bills. The serving staff never handled money and called out the final tally to the cashier who would take the cash and issue a handwritten receipt. Rose was a regular and given personal attention, which she enjoyed. She had cultivated a shop and telephone voice. It was quieter and more refined than at home. Inside the shop, Mr. Williams would come round from the counter to put items in her trolley, and they would exchange pleasantries. Rose would smile a lot and even laugh, which was not typical of her. The smell inside the shop could whet anyone's appetite. Cheese, coffee, newly baked pies, bacon. Everything was fresh and loose and weighed into strong brown paper bags that were reused at home.

Rose bought PG Tips loose leaf tea in four, quarter pound packets, or six if the children were on holiday from school. The packets were strong, colourful, and not easy to squash under the other shopping. Next on the list was four bags of Tate and Lyle sugar, 3 lbs of Windmill, Dutch unsalted butter, and a huge chunk of cheddar cheese, cut with a wire and wrapped in waxed paper. Bill adored cheese and would sneak to the fridge, break off a piece and take it to his comfy armchair in the living room to sit and savour. He was also an avid crossword puzzler, especially the big one in the *Daily Telegraph*, and as the newspaper manufacturing process cheapened, Rose would easily catch him out as he left tell-tale inky finger and thumb prints on the cheese left in the fridge. What great forensics! Two boxes of Omo detergent would be put in the bottom of a bag. The smell was exquisite—creamy clean, nose tickling soap. Other essentials on the weekly shopping list were Fairy household soap, Zamo disinfectant, several bottles of bleach, washing up liquid, Brillo pads and soft toilet rolls. Rose hated the staunch, water-repellent Izal toilet paper sheets.

The next shop would be the butcher. Bell's Butcher was quite an up-market establishment where customers often had their purchases delivered to their homes. Rose shopped there because she knew her meat. The quality was excellent, and she could ask for all the clever cuts. She was not fooled by expensive joints. She would buy the ham hocks discarded from other joints, which she soaked overnight to remove excess salt and then boiled with herbs, onions, and carrots. The resulting meat was as tasty as gammon. Rose accompanied the hock with potatoes and homemade pease pudding. This was made with yellow split peas and boiled like a suet pudding in a crisp white tea towel, reserved for that purpose. Mashed and mixed with a little milk and black pepper, it was nutritious and filling.

Rose was a regular customer there too, and Mr. Bell himself would serve her. He admired how she discussed what cut she wanted, and he would chop and trim the meat on the thick, worn, pitted wooden chopping blocks then place the succulence in thick, off-white paper, edges pulled away so he could display the finished article to Rose for approval before the final wrapping. He made his own fat juicy pork sausages that did not leak spitting water into the frying pan when mixed with hot fat. He once offered Rose beef sausages, which she refused in disdain. She considered beef sausages to be a cunning way to get rid of bits of beef that nobody would buy. She minced her own beef for cottage pie. Rose bought fresh farm eggs there. They were just inside the door, and she would pick them out herself. The egg boxes were reused each week.

The final visit was to the tobacconists at the bottom of the big hill. Rose would get the local weekly newspaper, Bill's two tins of Nosegay tobacco and three or four packs of Rizzla cigarette papers. Bill rolled his own cigarettes. She would sometimes treat herself to an aluminium tray of nut toffee, which came with a little disposable hammer to break the toffee into pieces. It was a lure that made the impending ascent up the big hill tolerable.

Daily necessities such as bread and greengrocery were bought locally. Rose loved fruit and the deep, floral patterned glass fruit bowl—strategically positioned on the sideboard—was always full of apples, oranges, and bananas. Teetering on top, on occasion, would be a proud pineapple. The greengrocers boiled their own beetroot in a big metal cauldron and whilst still warm, it would be wrapped in newspaper. Once home, the skin would slide off with the merest push, and it would be sliced. It was gorgeous. Fresh, flavoursome, and healthy. On a Saturday, Rose would despatch one of the children to buy five big loaves and a selection of seasonal vegetables for the weekend dinners. Often, a further loaf had to be bought on a Sunday at the Co-op Bakery, which sold bread straight from its ovens. Hand carts with ice brought fish and seafood to their customers, with the vendors calling out as they slowly edged along the roads, but without any local urchins following and begging for a chunk of ice. Those days were long past. Milk was delivered daily in bottles and had the gorgeous creamy top directly under the cap that caused many a fight amongst the children, all eager to claim it. Rose made her own ginger beer. She would buy a ginger root from the greengrocer and, like an apothecary concocting a special tonic, she would fill reusable glass bottles with the magic liquid and leave them to ferment in the top of the larder. Fresh from the bottle, the family would pour it onto ice cream and watch it fizz like a bonfire night sparkler before it was devoured and each bowl licked clean. Rose also used ginger root and rhubarb from the garden to make a luscious rhubarb and ginger jam.

Friday evening meant home-cooked fish and chips. Rose did a perfect size potato chip just using a sharp knife and a large potato. The deep fat fryer would be bubbling away on the gas cooker for at least an hour whilst the family were fed the piping hot meal. Rose left hers until last and would sit down with rosy cheeks and a stained apron from the heat and cooking oil, whilst Bill or one of the children made a cup of tea. Rose was adept at conveyor belt cooking. The family loved Shrove Tuesday, pancake day, and Rose would whip up a huge bowl of batter and cook individual pancakes. As each member of the family received their hot delicacy, they would sprinkle it with sugar, roll it up and squeeze fresh lemon juice on top before devouring it with relish. Before the first round was finished, the children would be clambering for more.

The gas cooker was a Cannon Icon. Made from white enamel, it had four gas rings of varying sizes and a large oven door that opened to reveal a second glass door through which you could see the food rising and browning. It also had an eyelevel grill. It was designed to shut away when not in use and had a button at the side which released it to collapse and fold. If it was not clicked back into place exactly right, it would refold when you moved the grill pan, even if it was already heating up. It was fortunate that cookers of this design did not grace the landings of the lodgings managed by landlords earlier in the century or many accidents would have occurred.

42

The telegram was expected. Rose's smile was so wide it almost hurt, and the furrows of hard work and long hours melted, albeit temporarily, from Bill's forehead. He took Rose by the hands and danced her round the kitchen floor—she was still embarrassed by an open show of emotion, but too happy to complain. They had won the football pools.

Bill was a gambler. His real joy was horse racing, followed closely by greyhound racing and in third place, the football pools, where he tried to predict which matches would result in a draw. He studied form before betting on horses, scouring the racing pages of the daily newspapers, making notes on pieces of paper that were blackened by the inky newsprint transferred from his fingers. Bill was pragmatic about his chances of winning and would not risk the scant family finances. Betting was an intellectual challenge. It stimulated a mind too easily diverted by the repetition of daily strife. His shift patterns allowed him some time to watch live afternoon meetings. He became animated and youthful, cheering and urging his horse on. If he won, he would punch an arm into the air with a "Yes!" and sit with a satisfied smile.

Often the bets were complex and would involve multiple races, so the tension would rise as each race was under starter's orders. Bill was in the zone. The family knew to stay silent. In later years, Bill opened a telephone account, and for a few hours each week, his world was complete—and without having to leave his comfy, well-worn armchair.

The football pools were entered weekly with mostly random numbers. Bill would ask each family member to choose a number. Sometimes he would write down all the numbers on scraps of paper and throw them on the floor. Each person present would pick a number and Bill would add some of his choices. Silence fell each Saturday afternoon. Seated in the living room, the family were rapt as the results were given top priority on the radio; crisp and distinct, but never hurried. That memorable afternoon in early 1953 when the magic eight score draws were confirmed, Bill's hand shook and his face glowed through tiny beads of perspiration. He dropped the pen several times, scrabbling with his fingers to pick it up without taking his eyes off the results he had written down in case they changed or disappeared. He beckoned Rose to check the results again together and they looked at each other in happy bewilderment.

The football pools paid out on dividends. Had Bill won the week before, the dividends were much higher that week. Bill was also part of a syndicate at work, so the winnings were shared. He did not dwell on the negatives. He and Rose were chuffed at their win, which the telegram confirmed was £800. They did not consider treating themselves. Holidays were for the wealthy. The money was spent on replacing well-worn furniture and beds, including a Beautility dining table and chairs with a sideboard, and just one luxury—a black and white television. It was a compact shiny black cabinet with a small screen at the top and big dials. The housing was Bakelite with a dark brown curly electrical lead and a plug that Bill had to fit. He spiked his finger with the screwdriver, which was routine whenever he attempted 'do it yourself'.

43

The small child held her brother's hand as they walked the short distance up the road to the primary school. It was September 1955. Rose and Bill's youngest child, Margaret, was heading to her first day at school—her brother had started there two years earlier. She looked and felt lost and bewildered but her mother did not think that it was important to take her youngest daughter to her first day of school personally and had delegated the task to her youngest son.

With the new freedom from the constraints of home and children, Rose seized the opportunity to secure a part-time job in a local café. She enjoyed the work and the social activity. In the early 1950s, there was still a tangible class system, and the café aspired to be upper-class and was called Chez Nous. The staff wore uniforms with small white lace-edged aprons and white lacy cotton hats. They were expected to speak to the customers with reverence, and Rose would use her telephone voice. The extra money was invaluable, and the staff shared the tips.

As she perfected running the house whilst working—another meticulously planned Army manoeuvre, adjusted seamlessly to recognise Bill's shift patterns—she left the café and went to work for a family that owned a chain of jewellers in the smart, expensive road that linked to Traps Hill. She loved her job in the big house. It utilised her skills as a house manager as her lady employer, Fanny, was often distracted and left Rose to manage their home life. Whilst Fanny painted—she was a talented artist and had paintings displayed in art galleries—socialised, played with her beloved Pekinese dogs and received visitors, Rose would ensure that the house functioned, was clean, and that a meal was ready in the evenings. Rose tolerated the snappy dogs, who seemed to like her, but who always went for the ankles if visitors entered their territory. Rose liked her employer. She was upper-class but kind and thoughtful, although her privileged upbringing had not included a lot of contact with the hoi polloi. The laundry was sent out, but without Rose, Fanny was unlikely to plan or execute an evening meal. Fanny and her husband were ecstatic with their housekeeper, but the problems for Rose's own family quickly mounted.

As she enjoyed life in the big house, the time she spent there increased exponentially. The children became 'latchkey' kids. Even if Bill was home, he could be asleep after a long shift. Rose was not abandoning the family but was side-tracked by these new experiences and attempted to fulfil her obligations to her own family by stringent organisation. Dinner would be prepared before she left in the morning, and it would sit in saucepans on the stove—mince and stews being easier during the week. Pies and roasts were relegated to weekends when she was home. She did a lot of baking on weekends, perhaps penitent, and there were cakes, apple pies and other titbits. If Bill was home and up, he would light the gas rings under the prepared saucepans. Otherwise, notes and instructions would be left for the older children to follow. One day, Bill salted the potatoes and greens before cooking them. It was the only time. Rose was not best pleased as she had already salted the pans, but how was Bill to know? From that day on, Rose would leave spilt salt on the saucepan lids to denote that the salt had been added.

At the outset, Rose worked at the big house part-time, but she soon became indispensable, and her working hours increased. Her wages, however, did not. Fanny loved her huge garden, and although she had a gardener, she pottered about in the garden and greenhouses and knew all about her plants and trees. With Rose's interest in flowers, they shared tips, and it wasn't long before Rose was working in the garden as well, pruning plants and picking fruit. One day, the gentleman of the house came home early to find Rose up a ladder in the garden with his wife standing at the bottom giving instructions. He admonished his wife. "Fanny, just what are you doing? We have a gardener. Let Rose off that ladder immediately and let her go inside to do what we employ her to do. I am so sorry, Rose. You should not be climbing ladders and pruning trees. I don't want you to have an accident, I would never forgive myself, and nor would Fanny."

"Of course, thank you," Rose replied. She was being polite as she had been secretly enjoying herself.

As Rose allowed the hours in the big house to lengthen, the family dinner time at home got later and later. At least there weren't any notes left to buy their dinner at the Pie and Mash shop. But it started to cause unhappiness at home and arguments. Bill would try to be supportive and understand that Rose was bringing in extra wages, but he could not support her staying so late, for no extra pay, just to ensure that the family at the big house got their dinner on time. She had almost become a live-in housekeeper and one of the children was often sent round to knock and remind her to come home.

In 1963, four years after she started working at the big house, the conflict was finally resolved. In September of 1963, Rose became seriously ill. The specialists and surgeons at the hospital were mystified and worked tirelessly to save her life. Tests were conducted, X-rays taken, and much discussion ensued. Rose's stomach became an artist's canvas with red and black lines drawn, closely resembling a London Underground map. Instead of stations being marked, however, it was internal organs. And instead of connecting train tracks, it was connecting veins. Knowing that time was running out, a decision was made to explore the kidneys, and in an ever-deteriorating condition, Rose was rushed into an operating theatre. Exploration of the kidneys proved fruitless, so in desperation they cut her open really wide, just as her appendix burst. It transpired that her appendix was on the wrong side, and Rose had developed peritonitis as a result of the unintended delay in an accurate diagnosis. It would have been a great episode of *Your Life in Their Hands*. Rose knew that she was a survivor and again she was proved right. If she had not been in the theatre when it burst, the surgeon was certain that she would have died. The family were bewildered that the almost useless 'worm-like appendage' of only a few inches in length that is the appendix could take someone's life.

Rose's stomach muscles did not survive the brutal slashing, and she was always conscious of the resultant flabbiness of the skin and complete loss of muscle tone. She would wear corsets for the rest of her life.

Fanny needed domestic help and employed someone else. Rose would not return to the big house but would become a Home Help within a team covering the local area. Home Helps were employed by the local council and had set days and hours, but with paid holiday, which she had never had before. Rose did light housework and shopping and true to form, in some households, got too involved. She was sent to help a young mother who had five children under three years of age. The mother had twins, then a little boy and now she had another set of twins. All the children had strabismus. She was fiercely house proud and had Rose moving wardrobes so that she could dust behind, but she would forget to feed the children and still had the newborns in carry cots on the kitchen table. Rose saw the dangers and the potential for unintended harm and felt unable to leave until the babies' father arrived home each day. Social Services had to be called in. She also had sad cases, like a nurse who had advancing multiple sclerosis and whose husband did not seem supportive. Rose grew to love a dear old lady who was reaching one hundred years of age. She lived in an ancient terraced house that still had gas lighting and a larder with a marble slab for the meat and cheeses. Rose would get her bits of shopping and make sure that she was eating, and they would have long chats when this was Rose's final visit of the day. Rose would chide her gently for sleeping on the settee at night and encourage her to keep her blood flowing by making the trip upstairs to her bedroom. Her family were local, but rarely visited. And then someone from the local newspaper heard about the gas lighting. A story emerged and there was a small party as electric lighting was installed. The old lady was ecstatic and not in least afraid of electricity. She loved to read, and the lighting was now perfect.

44

Over the next few decades, life for Rose and Bill would bring highs and lows, joy and trauma, but it would be real and vivid. The grey layers of war had cleared and were revealing a rainbow of opportunity.

They worked hard to provide for their family and increased financial demands resulted in even less time to nurture the children—or indeed their own relationship. Earning wages and the endless responsibilities in the home drained their emotional reserves, and although Bill tried to create a loving home environment, Rose was always too busy to nurture her children. The family was dysfunctional, and the siblings isolated even from each other.

Ellen, who adored her father, took to smoking cigarettes like Bill and, as young as fifteen years of age, felt she was in danger of being 'left on the shelf'. She married at seventeen. She had a complicated relationship with her mother, but Bill was always there for her. The three boys flourished in their careers, got married, bought their own houses and enjoyed the trappings of the middle-class. Being near to Rose and Bill was not high on their agendas. Their youngest daughter struggled with life and career and questioned for sixty years whether her mother loved her.

Rose, Bill, and the children were invited to the 90th birthday celebration of Granny Elizabeth Emily in 1958. Several bus rides later, they met a frail but alert Granny who got to see her great grandchildren, if only once. Rose and Bill attended Granny's funeral, after she died on the 18th of April, 1962, aged 94 years.

As the children left home, Rose and Bill finally had some quality time, and without a car, enjoyed coach holidays. Bill and Rose faced Bill's prostate cancer diagnosis and barbaric treatment: the only option in those days. The treatment burned the skin, and on one occasion, Bill did not reach the ward. His nostrils psychologically filled with smell of burning flesh as he arrived. He turned round and went home. Bill was also made redundant from the Gas Works and searched for employment. Only manual jobs were open to him, and these took a further toll on his health. Their retirement years brought them closer together, and they initially enjoyed retirement in Wiltshire, near Longleat, before moving back to Essex as Bill's health began to fail. Bill died of a massive heart attack, in hospital and surrounded by doctors in 1988, aged 73 years. Rose grieved and carved out a life that gave her contentment—she did not fear being alone. She continued to work in a local café into her mid-seventies.

Dementia impacted on Rose in her early nineties, and she moved into a nursing home for the final five years of her life from December 2015 to August 2020.

Ironically, dementia robbed Rose of both short and long-term memory, but released her deeply buried emotional vault. Her thorns were softened and allowed her to enjoy overt expressions of love and affection. She accepted kisses and cuddles as if they were routine. Rosie was reborn, if only for a year or two. Her youngest daughter, Margaret, witnessed the transformation and finally experienced the undivided attention of her mother. Did her mother love her? Neither Rose or Rosie could confirm.

Rose on her 100th *birthday*

Rosie had been denied her full potential, but Rose had bloomed and lived to one hundred years. On the 1st of August, 2020, she passed away peacefully from old age. Still in control, the nursing home staff were amazed at Rose's strength and her requests for a banana or a cup of tea during her lucid moments. She left when she was ready and not before.

A poem by Robert Frost, 1923

Nature's first green is gold,

her hardest hue to hold.

Her early leaf's a flower,

but only so an hour;

the leaf subsides to leaf,

so Eden sank to grief,

so dawn goes down to day.

Nothing gold can stay.

About The Author

Josie Bruce is a new author who will immerse you in her living worlds of sights, feelings and smells—physical and psychological. Born a *baby-boomer* in the summer of 1951, Josie was a lonely child who didn't have the opportunity to make friends. The youngest of five children, and with her parents working long hours to house and feed the family, she found solace in books and day-dreamed about becoming a ballerina, or perhaps a ballroom dancer. She had one talent, and that was writing, but it would take over sixty years to gain the confidence to share her writing with others. The moment is here. Josie writes about real people, believing that everyone's life is a story that could be told. *Together we make eternal memories.*